HOW TO MAKE EXTRA PROFITS IN TAXIDERMY

HOW TO MAKE EXTRA PROFITS IN TAXIDERMY

John E. Phillips

Winchester Press
An Imprint of New Century Publishers, Inc.

Printing Code

11   12   13   14   15   16

Library of Congress Cataloging in Publication Data
Phillips, John E.
  How to make extra profits in taxidermy.
  Includes index.

  I. Taxidermy industry.   II. Success in business.
I. Title
HD9999.T272 P49   1984   579'.4'068   84-10409
ISBN 0-8329-0345-0 (pbk)

DEDICATION

Resourcefulness is a virtue bred in the hour of desperation. Learning to look around and figure out what to do to keep the bill collectors from taking what you have inspires many to greatness. I discovered ways to make more money in taxidermy after close observation of a very willing teacher, my brother, William Archie Phillips, Jr.

When Archie needed money to buy gasoline for his car and had none, he looked at the options available to him. Someone mentioned that a research laboratory in our town was paying $25 apiece for monkey skulls. Knowing that the zoo had just destroyed several monkeys, Archie exhumed the corpses, cleaned and prepared the skulls, and acquired the needed gasoline money.

For years I watched that kind of resourcefulness bail him out of certain bankruptcy. So it is to him, William Archie Phillips, Jr., that I dedicate this book. Thanks for being a good brother.

ACKNOWLEDGMENTS

No work of any importance that lasts is ever done just by an individual, but is always the combined effort of several people. *How to Make Extra Profits in Taxidermy* holds ideas and suggestions that have been gleaned from thousands of sportsmen, taxidermists, and my family through the years. Work on this book could not have been completed without the diligent efforts of my wife, Denise; my mother-in-law, Marjolyn McLellan; Denise Huddleston; and Mike Hanley.

TABLE OF CONTENTS

FOREWORD

The old definition of taxidermy, "The art of preparing, stuffing, and mounting the skins of animals so as to appear lifelike," is no longer completely applicable to the trade today. This definition must be expanded to reveal a relatively new art form that includes the placement of specimens in habitat arrangements, the manufacture of jewelry, the tanning of skins, and 1,001 different skills that are encompassed under the title of taxidermist.

You can achieve some financial security by strict adherence to the dictionary definition of our art. However, hundreds of methods of acquiring additional revenue are available to the beginning, intermediate, or advanced taxidermist who wants to obtain more wealth by varying his outdoor skills and expanding.

This book has been compiled by a fellow laborer in our chosen art—not by a taxidermist who has all the answers on ways to make more money. The taxidermist who has a creative mind, a willingness to work, and a never-say-die attitude may find this book a springboard to launch into new areas of thinking that will increase the amount of money in his billfold at the end of the month after all the bills are paid.

Not all these techniques will work for all taxidermists in all situations. However, enough ways to make money are listed so an enterprising artist who uses and adapts the ideas to his particular area will greatly enhance his future in the taxidermy profession.

The book also contains many suggestions for making outdoor treasures that can either be given as gifts to friends and relatives or sold for a profit at shops, stores, yard sales, and bazaars. If you are looking for a way to enjoy outdoor sports and add dollars to the family budget through a parttime activity in which the whole family can participate, *How to Make Extra Profits in Taxidermy* is just what you need. You will be surprised how little money must be expended and how little effort made to create some fantastic outdoor treasures. My wife and children have helped with some of these money-making ideas. We have used by-products from our hunting and fishing trips for gifts as well as sources of income. We have had a lot of fun figuring out new and varying ways to use all that is in the outdoors as a source of income for our family.

HOW TO MAKE EXTRA PROFITS IN TAXIDERMY

As you obtain skill in taxidermy, you will be able to increase the amount of money you generate. However, even a newcomer can begin to make money. Start now to look for the things of beauty or unusual items in the outdoors and find a method of bringing them to the consumer.

(1) HOW TO FEATHER YOUR NEST. The wild turkey is one of the most beautiful of God's creations, with iridescent feathers that change colors as lights of varying intensities strike them. Black, bronze, brown, gold, and shades of green are all found within a single turkey feather. The feathers glow and sparkle like diamonds against the woodland floor as the light strikes them. And piling these feathers in the garbage seems an atrocity to the turkey hunter lucky enough to bag one.

A sportsman and his family have the potential to make hundreds of dollars from the by-product of this game animal. A proud gobbler presents many opportunities to a creative mind. Feathered jewelry always has been in vogue. A bit of glue, a few beads, some wire, and rawhide are all that is required to make lovely jewelry.

Check with your local craft store to obtain surgical posts for earrings, loops for necklaces, rawhide for headbands, and other materials that make beautiful jewelry with the addition of a feather.

And the turkey is by no means the only bird that sports striking plumage. Most waterfowl—such as the wood duck—also have excellent feathers for making jewelry. The bobwhite quail, ring-necked pheasant, and chukar partridge also are beautifully plumed. Before you begin to sell feathered jewelry in your area, however, check with your local

Two evenly-matched breast feathers from a gobbler, some beads from a craft store, eye hook, and surgical post are all that's required to make earrings such as these. The natural coloration of the plummage and the feathers' light-reflecting tendencies make for an eye-catching arrangement.

conservation officer to make sure this practice is not forbidden. If you find that the sale of feathered jewelry is prohibited, you have two options. Why not use this craft to produce gifts for Christmas, anniversaries, birthdays, weddings, or just to say thank you to a friend who has performed a kindness? Or you can order game birds from a game ranch with papers specifying their domestic status, which will allow you to sell the feathered products in most states.

(2) THE OTHER END OF THE FEATHER BUSINESS. Although the feathers of many fowl have been used for making jewelry for years, one enterprising entrepreneur found his gold mine in bird's manure. A quail rancher by trade, this sportsman walked by his quail pens each day and not only inspected the birds he was raising, but noticed the multitude of droppings they left in the yard. If Frank O. Hill of Union, South Carolina, had had but a little creativity, he would have developed a method of selling the manure for fertilizer or some other agricultural purpose. But Hill had that rare spark of genius that allowed him to see beauty and symmetry in the common and ordinary. Hill looked at the quail dung, picked it up, and admired its formation and color. He decided that this was something more than fertilizer. Nature had created a piece of art that completely had gone unnoticed for years until he discovered it with his questioning eye. By encasing the quail stools in clear plastic, he produced cuff links, tie tacks, stick pins, and every other type of jewelry imaginable. Today he ships his quail stool products around the world. To obtain a catalogue of these products, contact Frank O. Hill, Pine Hill Game Farm, Rt. 5, Dept. WH, Union, SC 29379, (803) 427-8795.

(3) PLASTIC TAXIDERMY PRODUCES MORE DOLLARS. Quail droppings are not the only beautiful oddities in nature. Insects, butterflies, small snakes, leaves, and 101 other things can be encased in plastic to form jewelry, paperweights, and attractive desk-top pieces for your taxidermy customers. Deep Flex Plastic Molds, Inc., P.O. Box 11471, Fort Worth, TX 76110, sells the plastic and molds you will need.

The procedure for imbedding items in clear plastic is simple. Pour the plastic into the mold until the mold is halfway filled. Wait for the plastic to become tacky, then place the specimen you want encased upside down on top of the plastic. Next, pour in a new batch and wait for the resin to harden.

Ashtrays and desk mountings are not the only molds available for clear-plastic taxidermy. One person purchased a mold for a toilet seat. He poured the mold half full of plastic, then laid small snakes, bugs, and grasshoppers into the plastic. His finished product caused both shrieks of laughter and screams of horror in his restroom.

The only limiting factor in plastic taxidermy is one's own creativity. Squirrel and beaver skulls that have been whitened with bleach make interesting paperweights. The list goes on and on, so if you are looking for more money in taxidermy, the plastic mount is an excellent place to start.

(4) THE TURKEY—OPTING NOT TO STUFF HIM. Even if a turkey hunter does not choose to have his gobbler mounted, he will save the feet, beard, and tail in most cases. The tail is usually spread, then the tail, beard, and feet are allowed to dry. After a few years, these trophies are often relegated to the garage or the back of some closet or drawer and eventually may rot. But by mounting the parts of a turkey hunter's trophy in an attractive display, you can make more money and provide a needed service to him.

The tail and feet must be preserved to ensure that decay and insects will not destroy them. Acquire a large hypodermic needle from either your local drugstore or a feed store that carries veterinarian supplies. Fill the syringe with a solution like Instant Mounting Fluid, which can be obtained from Taxidermy Supply Co., 5011 E. Texas, Bossier City, LA 71111. Inject Instant Mounting Fluid into the fleshy part of the tail. Next, spread the tail on a large piece of cardboard or wood and use either pins or nails to hold it in place. Store the tail in a warm, dry area so it will dry in the proper position.

Inject the turkey's feet along the tendon in the back of the leg, the palm of the foot, and each toe. Lay the feet on their sides, curling the toes together like your hand looks when it is cupped and all of the fingers are touching one another. Let the turkey's foot dry until it becomes rigid. Put borax on the meat attached to the beard and put it in the same place to dry.

Once the specimens are dry, make a covering for the butt of the tail using velvet. Red or green seem to be the colors most preferred by customers. An ideal velvet covering, a skullcap, can be purchased from the San Angelo Co., Inc., P.O. Box 984, San Angelo, TX 76902.

If you are blessed with woodworking skills and can create your own panels on which to attach the tail, feet, and beard, do so by all means. If not, choose a panel offered by any of the taxidermy supply houses. These panels will come already finished. All you have to do is add a hanger to the back.

To attach the turkey's tail to the panel, I use nails and hot glue. A hot-glue gun can be obtained from a local hardware store or most taxidermy supply houses. Place the tail in the center and a little high on the panel with the velvet covering over the butt. Then attach the turkey feet on either side of the mounted tail by using one of the strong instant glues that can be purchased at most hardware and discount stores. Mount the beard just below the tail. A small piece of rawhide also may be glued over the butt of the leg to hide the bone and the meat of the beard and make a more attractive mount. The material cost for mounting this trophy is nominal, but the retail and aesthetic values are high.

Another option that can be offered to the hunter to help you make

Even if the turkey you tagged didn't have a 9-inch beard or pass the 20-pound mark, you can still make a fine display of the tail such as this. It's simple and presents a tasteful and decorative mount. The feathers here indicate a mature bird, but even a jake can be turned into a similar display. The velvet cap and wooden panel add to the piece, but you can experiment with different arrangements to suit your taste.

additional revenue from turkeys is adding the wings to the tail/foot/beard combination. To preserve each wing, make an incision on the underside, then pull the skin back leaving the muscle and bone exposed. Remove the muscle from the bone, leaving the skin intact. Sprinkle borax in the incision, rubbing it well into the skin and along the bone below the incision. Next, use cotton to replace the tissue that was removed and sew up the incision with braided nylon casting line or quilting thread.

Thoroughly inject the rest of the wing—from the incision to the tip—using a hypodermic syringe and Instant Mounting Fluid. Stretch the wing out and allow it to dry. Use the same procedure on the other wing.

Once the wing is dry, dust it off. Prior to placing the turkey's tail on the large mounting panel, attach the wings by running wires from the back side of the panel over and around the wings and back through the panel. Twist the wire firmly to ensure that the wings remain secure. Next, mount the tail in the center of the panel and slightly high, overlapping part of the wings. Flank the tail with the preserved feet.

If the sportsman wants to go one step further, you can make a small incision in the velvet covering for the tail and glue in the turkey's beard. Try this method several times on your own turkeys or those of close friends before you attempt it commercially.

Since the real trophies of an old gobbler are his spurs and beard, the thinking taxidermist will offer yet another mount that is less expensive than those already mentioned. Inject the turkey's feet with Instant Mounting Fluid. Put the toes together and curve the feet to the desired position. Then apply borax to the meat on the beard.

When the feet and beard are dry, use a piece of rawhide or deerskin to cover the ends of the leg and the meat on the beard. You can use clear shellac to coat the feet and make them shine, if you wish, or leave them natural. Purchase or make a finished panel. Then use either hot glue or instant glue to attach the feet on either side of the small panel. In the center of the panel, glue the beard above the feet. Then place a brass, engraved nameplate on the panel. This plate should have the hunter's name, the date he took the bird, how much the gobbler weighed, and the place it was killed. Now the outdoorsman has a unique, inexpensive trophy to hang on his wall that will remind him of the day he downed the tom. And you will have more dollars in your pocket for creating the mount.

Still another option to preserve the turkey's spurs is to saw them off the turkey's leg. Glue a jeweler's clasp to the butt of the spur, then attach earring wires to the clasp to fashion a pair of spur earrings for the sportsman's wife. Paint the spurs with shellac or clear gloss to make them shiny. Or, remove the spurs from the leg of the turkey and use them as tips for bolo ties, tie tacks, cuff links, and centerpieces for belt buckles or necklaces. The creative taxidermist can fashion beautiful and unusual jewelry from an old gobbler's battle gaffs.

(5) DEER FEET CAN PAW UP EXTRA DOLLARS. Each year

Looks impressive, doesn't it? You may not have a braggin'-size rack for the trophy room, but the deerfoot gun rack below the head mount can be just as attractive, and more practical. The ingredients are easier to come by—all deer have feet, but not too many hunters find critters with 8-point racks.

thousands of deer feet are thrown away by sportsmen who fail to see the value in the cloven hooves of the whitetail deer, mule deer, and elk. These feet can be washed, preserved, and made into many useful items

To make a deerfoot rack or other mount using the feet, first wash the feet in detergent to remove dirt, grime, and blood.

Cut the hoof off about five inches from the first joint above the hoof. You don't need a power saw as shown here, but it makes the job easier.

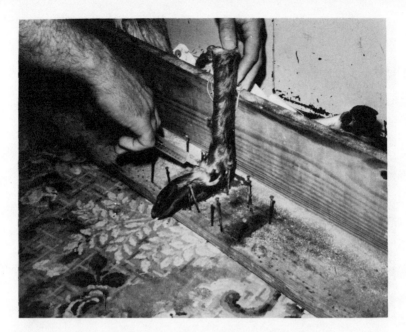

Inject the foot poison solution mentioned in the text between the two dew claws.

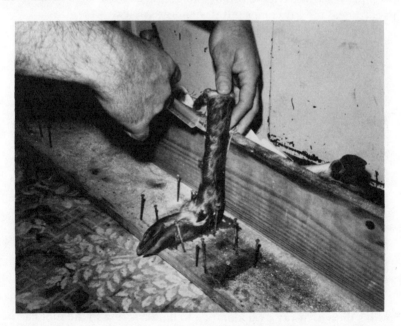

The solution is also injected halfway up the leg as shown here.

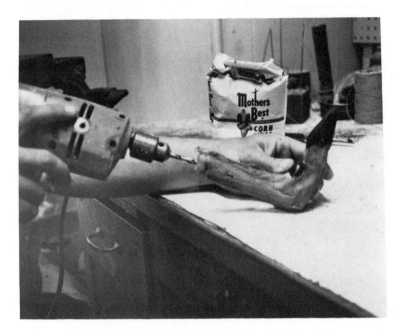

Drill out the bone marrow from the deerfoot. Now pack cornmeal into the empty marrow cavity to remove all grease and continue drilling out the cornmeal until it comes out dry and greaseless.

Now it's time to insert a wooden peg to hold a screw so the foot can be mounted on a board.

Hangers like these, available at nearly any hardware or frame store, are placed on the back of the wooden panel.

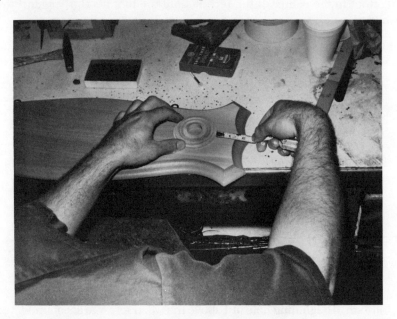

Measure and secure wooden ferrules or braid to the panel.

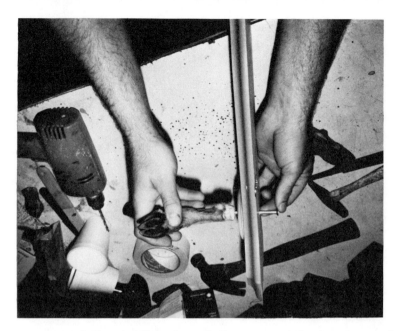

Now you can drill a $^1/_4''$ hole through the center of the ferrule into the panel. Insert a $2^1/_2''$ No. 10 wood screw into the peg and screw the deerfoot to the center of the ferrule until the foot fits flush against the wood.

Drill a small beginning hole just above the wood screw to accommodate a nail, as shown, to add strength.

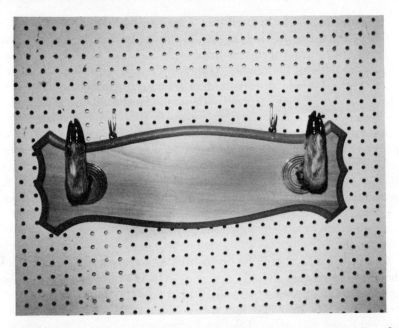

The finished gun rack, or clothes and hat rack, is an attractive piece for the deer hunter.

including gun racks, letter openers, knife handles, thermometers, and hat racks.

Two techniques work well for treating deer hooves:

1. Split the leg to the hoof and remove the bone and cartilage. Preserve the skin by rubbing on a dry preservative that can be purchased from most taxidermy supply houses. Insert a foot form and sew the skin back together. Use clear lacquer to paint the toenails and dewclaws to make the hooves shine and take on an added luster. After the hooves have dried, they can be attached to panels and made into various articles.

2. Another method that works, but is not as lasting as the foot form technique, is to inject the foot and the leg with a mixture of Instant Mounting Fluid and borax. Add about one handful of dry powdered borax to one quart of Instant Mounting Fluid and stir until the borax is dissolved. With a hypodermic needle inject the hoof and leg with enough preservative to dry all the skin. Do not overinject to the point that the hoof begins to balloon. Set the hoof in the desired position and permit it to dry until hard.

13

After the foot is well dried, use a quarter-inch bit to drill out the marrow from the center hole of the bone in the back of the leg. Pack the hole with dry cornmeal and continue to drill the foot until the cornmeal comes out without being oily. Next, whittle a piece of hardwood and drive it into the hole. Now your deer feet are ready to be attached by placing a screw through a panel and into the hardwood inside the bone.

Discarded deer feet can also be made into stylish lamps. These lamps can be custom designed to fit the individual sportsman's taste. An inexpensive lamp can be made from a single foot, or a lamp can be crafted with four feet. The lamp itself can consist of either a single or double socket, and the shade can be chosen from several styles to personalize the lamp even more. If the sportsman enjoys hunting ducks, elk, bear, or deer, an appropriate lampshade can be selected. If he is a bass fisherman or a trout angler, lampshades are available with pictures of these fish.

The taxidermist should be aware that a custom-designed lamp and shade will bring a much higher price from the hunter who acquired the feet than from an individual who did not take the deer.

Ashtrays made from elk's feet are also interesting conversation pieces and excellent gift items. Elk-foot fittings are relatively inexpensive, removing the bone and inserting the fitting is an easy task. An ashtray can then be glued to the top of the fitting. For a very low cost the taxidermist in search of new dollars can create an unusual novelty item that will please his customers and bring him more business.

Van Dyke Supply Co., in Woonsocket, SD 57385, probably has the best catalog of supplies and accessories for crafting deer's feet. If you will mention the type of deer-foot item you want to build, they will be more than happy to send the supplies you need to complete the article. These deer-foot products can be sold at gift shops, sporting goods stores, trade fairs, and garage sales to provide extra income. However, be sure to check local state regulations regarding the sale of such items.

Deer feet are easy to acquire if you hunt or know a group of hunters who bag deer regularly. And you may be able to trade finished deer-foot products for raw deer feet with which to work.

(6) SELL TO MODERN-DAY MOUNTAIN MEN. The early pioneers of this country used all that was wild to make a living. They were trappers, hunters, and fishermen. Their clothing and jewelry came from the woods and waters. To be a mountain man, you had to have a buckskin suit. Most of the time the buckskin was tanned by the Indians, then smoked over willow branches to add color. The leather was cut and fitted to the frontiersman and was held together and adorned with different natural products such as horns and rawhide.

Any mountain man worth his salt wore some kind of cap or hat. Although Daniel Boone's coonskin cap and Davy Crockett's ring-tailed hat have received the most publicity, many woodsmen sported coyote, fox, or skunk caps. The most popular and serviceable, however, was probably the beaver cap. Like today's cowboy hats, a hat in pioneer days

With the growing interest in muzzleloader hunting and authentic costumes of days gone by, the taxidermist can readily find an eager market for items such as this hunter's beaver-skin hat, angler-handle knife, and cow-horn powder container.

was just another hat without some kind of ornament. Mountain men adorned their head coverings with bear claws, bleached hawk skulls, coon tails, eagle feathers, or mountain lion teeth.

The typical mountain man also carried a black powder rifle, often in a fringed buckskin sheath. The fringe was not for decoration, but rather allowed the buckskin to dry quicker after getting wet. The mountain man's knife and tomahawk also sported buckskin covers. His leggings and moccasins were custom made and allowed him to glide across the woodland floor without popping twigs or cracking limbs. From the top of his hat to the sole of his moccasins, the mountain man wore apparel and carried items that were manufactured by a pioneer taxidermist.

The idea of self-sufficiency and testing one's raw will against the elements still flourishes in our society today. Many believe that the mountain man's way of life, attitude of self-reliance, and ability to live off the land are worthwhile goals for the twentieth century. These values have spawned a new breed of mountain men who are searching for and requiring many of the same products that the men they emulate used every day. They are a new breed of customers for the keen-eyed taxidermist who can determine their needs and supply a product they want.

Interesting necklaces or earrings for mountain men can be made from the toenails and dewclaws of deer hooves. By sawing off the deer's toenails and removing the dewclaws, a craftsman may have some very valuable items to sell at a mountain man rendezvous or trade fair. If you have access to a rock or cartridge tumbler, put the toenails or dewclaws into the machine to polish them to a high luster. If a tumbler is not readily accessible, clear gloss will work equally well.

Once the toenails have been either polished or glossed, small eyes or loops may be screwed into or glued onto each toenail. A chain can be passed through these eyes to make a necklace. Surgical posts can be used for making earrings from dewclaws. All these supplies may be purchased at local craft stores or jewelry shops.

Other trinkets extremely fashionable for today's modern mountain men are buttons made from deer horns, custom-made deerskin clothing, and animal skulls. Deer-horn buttons are not hard to make. Saw off a deer antler to the desired button size. Then use a small bit to drill four holes for the thread that holds the button to the garment. These buttons may sell for as much as fifty cents apiece, and one good deer antler can produce as many as 100 buttons.

To obtain information on the needs and wants of these modern-day mountain men, write to the associations listed below. Also inquire about publications in which you can advertise your wares:

American Mountain Men
P.O. Box 259
Lakeside, CA 92040

National Association of Primitive Riflemen
Box 885
Big Timber, MT 59011

National Muzzle Loading Rifle Association
Box 67
Friendship, IN 47021

(7) BECOME A HIDE TANNER. My experience has been that tanning your own hides is extremely time consuming, messy, cold, hard work. Like many other taxidermists, I decided to tan skins some years ago, but I found the amount of labor required to produce a quality, finished skin was unbelievable. I used every tanning recipe that anybody suggested or that I could find in the library. I discovered no shortcuts to home tanning until a product called Tannit was introduced. This product is described in Chapter 69 of this book.

Very few taxidermists tan their own hides. Those who bill themselves as "tanners" actually take in deer hides and ship the skins to large tanneries throughout the country. So you may find a good job opportunity as this kind of tanner in your area. The only materials required are a freezer, a fleshing beam, which you can make yourself, and a fleshing tool you can order from most taxidermy supply houses. You will need salt and a dry place to store the hides as well as a quality tanner to whom you can ship your salted skins. If you decide to get into this area of work, there are a few pitfalls to watch:

1. Make sure you charge enough to make a profit on each hide. Count fleshing time, salting, boxing, shipping both ways, handling, tanning cost, and secretarial work.
2. Always send a few extra hides in case something happens to one. You usually can offer a customer an already-tanned hide if his is ruined.
3. Choose a good tannery. Several tanneries in the nation do top quality work, but some are questionable. Inquire as to which are most reputable and use them even if the price is a little higher so you will be sure your skins are treated properly.

My own experience has proven that getting a quality tan on your skins with home tanning processes is next to impossible and takes too much time to yield a reasonable profit.

A taxidermist can make money as a tanner if he does not underprice his work. If you cannot make a profit producing tanned skins, you are charging too little. A customer willing to pay your price to have his hide tanned can become a valuable asset to your business and bring you other work.

For more information on tanning, consult:

American Fur Dressing Co.
10816 Newport Hwy.
Spokane, WA 99218

Beca Furs
Rt. 1, Box 2
Sturgis, MS 39769

Clearfield Taxidermy
603-605 Hannah St.
Clearfield, PA 16830

Colorado Fur Tanning and Fur Dressing Co.
1787 S. Broadway
Denver, CO 80223

E.L. Heacock Co., Inc.
Gloversville, NY 12078

New Method Fur Dressing Co.
131 Beacon St.
South San Francisco, CA 94080

(8) BECOME A CUSTOM GARMENT COMPANY. If you enjoy the sport of trapping or if you have friends who trap, you may be able to acquire some fur for the manufacture of custom fur coats. Do not worry if you do not possess the skill or know-how to tan hides or manufacture garments. Your responsibility is to get the skins, take the measurements, and send the information and hides to a furrier where the garments can be made. Beaver, fox, opossum, raccoon, coyote, otter, and skunk make luxurious fur garments. Some furriers even may sell you the fur as well as make the garment for you if you have problems acquiring suitable skins.

Write Beca Furs, Rt. 1, Box 2, Sturgis, MS 39769, to obtain a wholesale price list as well as a retail suggested price list on their custom furs. They also will provide you with all the information you need on caring for raw skins, shipping skins, taking measurements, and other pertinent advice for your custom garment business. A good trapper who can catch his fur, sell his customer on selecting the fur for a coat, and work with a furrier to produce a high-quality, custom-made garment that can open up a new and relatively untouched market in the fur industry.

But the fur business is not the only custom apparel opportunity available to sportsmen in search of added income. Thousands of deerskins are thrown away each year, because the lack of demand for the leather and the problems arising from trying to ensure a steady supply are often insurmountable. However, the taxidermist who can collect deer hides, flesh them, salt them, and ship them can develop a custom apparel market. Two good companies to investigate in this market are:

Custom Coat Co., Inc.
227 N. Washington St.
Berlin, WI 54923

Licardo Gloves
27 Montgomery St.
Gloversville, NY 12078

I have dealt with both these companies. They will be happy to send you catalogs and information to show you how to prepare skins for tanning. They will also give you a cost breakdown on the garments and any other needed details that will help your deerskin business become a success.

But if you, a friend, or a neighbor wants to manufacture deerskin or fur clothing, you should be warned about some things in advance:

1. Most home sewing machines are not equipped for sewing leather. You may have to invest in a special machine and special needles.
2. A large amount of cutting and sewing is required to make a coat.
3. Your best bet may be to design and make mountain men's clothing because the sewing is done with rawhide or nylon.

(9) TURN SKINS INTO RUGS. Deer, raccoon, fox, bobcat, coyote, bear, and wolf skins can all be turned into artistic area rugs that will be conversation pieces. Salt, dry, and ship the skins to a tannery. The pelts will be tanned with a high luster and made into a soft, pliable leather with the hair still attached. To make these pelts into expensive-looking area rugs, sew the holes in the skin, then sew the skin to a backing of rug batting and felt.

Area rugs with the animal's head mounted also have become increasingly popular over the past few years. Using a head mount, ear

By working with a custom garment company, you can add customers who are looking for this type of special work. This custom possum-skin coat was made by Beca Furs in Sturgis, Mississippi, from skins collected by sportsmen and taken to their local taxidermist.

A natural beaver-skin coat such as this is made possible by combining the talents and efforts of a sportsman-trapper, a taxidermist, and a custom garment company.

liners, and a jaw set, you can fashion a rug with all the realism of the wild creature.

Van Dyke Supply Co., Woonsocket, SD 57385, offers an inexpensive book (under $5.00) entitled *Rug Making*. These simple instructions can help you turn tanned skins into attractive rugs that may be sold to interior decorators, given as presents, or placed around your house or office to demonstrate your work.

One year we had 15 extra deer hides tanned. Then, when work was slack, we backed, felted, and sewed the hides to make area rugs. These rugs were displayed to show our customers what could be done with their deerskins instead of throwing them in the garbage can. The rugs were also sold to interior decorators and given as presents to influential sportsmen in the region who referred other hunters to us.

Of course, one of the problems associated with rug manufacturing is obtaining the pelts. Often you may have customers who would like to have a rug mounted but do not have the specimen. Work with a reliable trapper in your area. He will be a good source for not only animal skins, but any other animals you may need in the taxidermy business. Keeping a few extra critters in your freezer is not a bad idea. If a client comes in with a specimen too badly shot up to be mounted or with hair slippage, you may be able to offer another coon, fox, or bobcat in exchange and thereby save the mount. I generally charge the customer the same price the trapper charges me for exchange specimens. Although I do not make any extra money from selling the hide, I really score with customers. Also, a trapper may help supply you with driftwood to use in mounting animals and birds.

Skin rugs tanned with the hair on are soft and beautiful and should not be overlooked as a possible source of income.

(10) DEERSKIN SCRAPS. Often deerskins will be brought to you that have large holes in them, the hair rubbed off from being dragged through the woods, or bullet burns that make them unsuitable for the rug market. Before you throw them away, stop for a minute and consider another often-overlooked market in which a person with piecing and quilting skills may be able to turn large profits. These less-than-prime deerskins can be cut into pieces and sewn together to make a beautiful bedspread.

One of the most unusual spreads I have ever seen was pieced together using the white underbelly of a deer as a center and white triangles going out from that center to the four corners of the spread. Except for the head of the bed, the entire outside edge of the spread was made up of tanned, flat deerskins. The spread was both unusual and extremely warm—heavy and beautiful. Area rugs and throw pillows can be made by using this same quilting technique.

You don't have to live in a bachelor pad to have use for a skin rug such as this. The display makes an attractive and rugged trophy for any game room, library, or den.

The sportsman who enjoys the beauty of tanned, dyed buckskin may prefer to have his pelts tanned with the hair off, then dyed different colors and pieced together to make intricate quilting designs. Glovers' needles prove to be the most useful for sewing the leather. These needles can be obtained from most taxidermy supply houses.

Pieces of tanned deerskin with the hair off can also be used to cover the bases of deer, elk, and moose horns in mounts. Another use of the buckskin is to cover the butt of turkey feet and beards. You will find 101 other purposes for tanned deer leather with the hair off, so keep several pieces on hand in your taxidermist's shop.

When we get through with these scraps, we sometimes put them into plastic bags and sell them for $1.50 to $2.00 per bag. Just because we do not know what to do with these remnants doesn't mean that someone else who comes into our office won't have ideas. Customers buy these small bags of scrap leather and take them home to be fashioned into who knows what.

I know of one taxidermist who had some of his extra skins made into buckskin and dyed different colors. He then cut them up into odd-shaped pieces, put the pieces into plastic bags, and offered them for sale. He discovered he made more money selling scrap leather than he did selling the hides in whole pieces.

The entire salvage industry is made up of people who have learned how to do something with other people's discards. Too often we in taxidermy fail to realize that a lot of the material we throw out could be turned into dollars if offered for sale.

(11) THERE IS MONEY IN THE TAIL. Thousands of deerskins are thrown away each year, and even more squirrel hides come to rest in garbage cans. But attached to each one of these hides may be the potential for a $1.00 to $10.00 for the sportsman with a keen eye.

Lures made from a buck's tail always have caught a variety of fish. Traditionally the bucktail jig has been a bait preferred by bass and crappie fishermen around the country. However, most jig manufacturers have a difficult time finding enough deer tails to make their jigs. They are willing to pay for these by-products of your hunting and taxidermy. Cut the tails off the hides, then split and salt them. You can sell them to commercial customers for ten to fifty cents each. However, you may find a higher-priced market with local bait manufacturers in your area. If you are looking for still greater profits, consider pouring your own lead-headed jigs, painting them, wrapping the bucktails to the jig heads, and marketing your own lures.

Any pan fisherman will tell you the value of the squirrel-tail jig. These little jigs resemble small animals, and panfish just cannot seem to resist them. Both fox and grey squirrel tails are used in the manufacture of these jigs.

Although no one will ever get rich selling squirrel or deer tails, you will be surprised at how many extra dollars you can pick up from what hunters throw away. And if you decide to make your own jigs from deer or squirrel tails, you may develop a lucrative home business provided you can keep enough tails on hand.

The following companies buy deer tails. Before sending them any, however, inquire as to their needs and prices by writing to:

Adirondack Taxidermy Studios
Greenfield Center, NY 12833

Passloff, Inc.
28 W. 38th St.
New York, NY 10018

Squirrel tails are purchased by Sheldon's Inc., P.O. Box 508, Antigo, WI 54409.

One of the best ways to get the most out of these tails may be a trade or barter system. I have found that I come out much better by trading tails for finished lures that I can sell than by taking money for the tails from lure manufacturers. The price a taxidermist receives for raw tails is not nearly as high as what he can make selling finished lures that a local bait manufacturer gives him in exchange for tails. Very few hairs are required to make a bucktail or a squirrel-tail jig. One good deer tail may make 10 to 20 jigs. If the jig maker gives you three to five jigs per tail and you sell the jigs for fifty to seventy-five cents each, you will make more than if you had been paid for the tails.

Mountain men represent another lucrative market for tails. A good deer tail that has been tanned can be sold to a mountain man as a trailer for a hat or to Indians for use in their costumes. The deer tail is a lovely ornament for many things. It is valuable if you can determine how to use it best.

(12) PAINT YOUR SKINS. Another beautiful art form—that goes back to the first Americans—is painting on deerskin. The Indians found that deerskin paintings were an excellent way to record history and made interesting decorations for their homes as well as good trade items. Even if you do not have an artistic flair of your own, you can acquire the hides and still produce a saleable item. First, have your deerskins tanned with the hair off. Find an artist who will paint an outdoor scene—such as a buck and a doe drinking from a stream, wild ducks exploding off the water, or a stately elk bugling from a mountain top—on the smooth side of the skin. These skins can be stretched with rawhide over a tree-limb frame, much as the Indians once did, to add a rustic effect to the painting.

Or, once you have acquired a painted skin, it may be sold by itself and merely tacked to a wall, or stretched like a canvas and placed in a

Here's a new twist for your tanned hides... a little wildlife art to decorate the "canvas" is an unusual touch that can add sales to your business.

finished wooden frame. Unpainted deerskins with the hair off also can be sold to artists for use in imaginative paintings.

Paintings on skins tanned with the hair on are also in demand. For instance, a black line drawing of a hound with a coon up a tree on the hide side of a coonskin makes a cherished gift for a coonhunter. This piece of art can be personalized even more by tanning the hide from the coon that the sportsman's dog has treed. Paint the picture on the skin and enter under the painting words like "Treed by Ole Blue, December 2, 1982." The skin can then be either stretched and framed or tacked to the wall. And do not forget the fox hunter. Tanning and painting skins will also appeal to the customer who chases the wily fox with hounds. All hides can be used in this manner for special, personalized gifts for sportsmen at Christmas or on birthdays, as well as for the sheer aesthetic enjoyment of the art.

(13) THERE ARE DOLLARS AT MOO U. If you live in a college town or if there is a college nearby, a good source of revenue can be found just inside the hallowed halls of ivy. Fraternities will bet other chapters at

rival schools on the outcome of football and basketball games. One of the favorite objects of a wager is a tanned cowhide with the hair on. At the end of the game the losing chapter sends the winning fraternity a hide. On the skin side of the hide—burned or painted into the leather—is the score and the date of the game.

A thinking sportsman will talk with these fraternities and attempt to become the supplier of the hides and lettering. An agreement for the next year should be reached between the taxidermist and the fraternity right after football or basketball season is over. In this way the taxidermist will have the time required to find a local slaughterhouse that can supply him with the green skins. Then all he will have to do is flesh and salt the skins and ship them to the tannery. The tanned hides should return prior to the upcoming season, giving the taxidermist time to locate a person to do the burning or lettering on the back sides of the hides if he does not have these skills himself.

Cowhides also are a tremendous source of revenue to keep around your shop. Lovely skins in various hues, from different breeds of cows, add color and luxury to dens, mountain cabins, and second homes. A well-tanned cowhide is often an interior decorator's dream. These professionals may pay well for your hides, so take the time to visit their offices and show them the quality of a finished skin. Once the interior decorator knows that tanned cowhides are available locally, he will suggest these types of area rugs more readily to his clients.

(14) SLAUGHTERHOUSE BONANZA. Your local slaughterhouse may be a gold mine waiting to be discovered. Here you have an opportunity to select your hides before the animals are butchered and often pick up unusual discards that can be turned into dollars.

And if a dog-food factory is close by, check the old horses. Often they bear beautiful hides that can be tanned, hair off, and made into expensive-looking area rugs. One of the most unique hides we ever tanned was that of a 13-year-old Appaloosa horse. The fleshing and salting process required a lot of effort and a large work area. But once the huge white skin with brown spotted markings was tanned, it was a magnificent addition to our customer's trophy room. Until that time I had never thought of a horse's hide as a decorative piece. But I must admit that I regretted turning the lovely skin over to its owner when he paid the bill.

Even goat skins can be attractive and often are sold as rugs. A domestic goat skin looks just as exotic as a wild goat skin when draped across a chair or hung on a wall. Cow feet—polished and made into ashtrays—and cow tails—skinned, preserved, and mounted on a board— make good novelties and gag gifts. Cow horns, cleaned and polished, are perfect for a mountain man's powder horn.

One of the main reasons that more livestock producers do not salvage hides and horns is that they fail to recognize the beauty of the animals' pelts and the many uses of their horns. An enterprising taxidermist can select a large winter pelt from the beef cattle at a slaughterhouse, then have the skin tanned to hang in the office of the slaughterhouse. This will accomplish two things. It will provide an unusually decorative wall hanging for the owner of the slaughterhouse and give the taxidermist an excellent way to advertise his hide business.

Since most slaughterhouses sell the hides of the animals they butcher, the taxidermist must offer to compensate the owner for any customers referred to him. Or, possibly, you could trade him a finished hide for a certain number of clients he refers. Another excellent method of making friends and acquiring pelts at a slaughterhouse is to tan a goat skin or some other small skin for the workers actually doing the slaughtering. Perhaps if one of the workers comments on what a pretty hide an animal has and how nice it would look tanned, the slaughterhouse's customers will also become taxidermy customers. Working very closely with the owner and workers in the slaughterhouse may create a whole new business for the taxidermist.

Likewise, a slaughterhouse is an excellent place to acquire cattle hides to use as imitation bear hides. Most people cannot tell the difference between the skins. Larry Blomquist of Hammond, Louisiana, explains:

> During the winter I go to slaughterhouses and look for thick-coated, large, black Angus cattle. The winter hair of the black Angus is almost identical to that of a bear. I purchase these hides and have them tanned. Most of the time I sell the hide as is, once it is tanned. I tell my customers what the hide is and what it looks like. Then when they take the black hide home and put it on the floor, most of the time we two are the only ones who know that they do not have a real bear hide lying in front of their fireplace. Now if they want us to, we'll cut the hide in the shape of a bear skin and they really have a trophy to show off.

A prime black Angus hide, well tanned with the hair on and beautifully displayed, will be a prize for your customer and open up a new market for you.

With a little creativity and imagination, a person in our profession can walk into a slaughterhouse, pick up some discarded animal parts for a few dollars, and, with proper care and treatment, turn them into lucrative articles for sale.

(15) PULL A JAW AND TURN A DOLLAR. Almost every deer hunter would like to know the age of his deer. By spending just a bit of time with the game biologist in your state you can learn to tell a deer's age by its

jawbone. Determining the age of your customers' deer will help you become an authority on deer in your area and thereby increase the amount of traffic in your shop.

Plaques displaying jawbones of various ages can be made and sold to sportsmen and hunting clubs for prices ranging from $5.00 to $25.00. After you have skinned a deer for mounting, separate the lower jaw into two halves and clean each half. Use indelible ink to write the age on the jawbone. Make sets of jawbones with ages ranging from one to six years and glue them to a finished wooden plaque that can be hung in a hunter's den or at his hunting club. If you prefer to give these plaques away, be sure to attach an advertising decal or business card to ensure future business.

(16) DENTURES OF DEATH. The very word *shark* strikes fear into many a coastal sportsman. The movies that have been made about shark attacks, as well as the books and magazines that have shown the damage wrought by slashing teeth, constantly bring our attention to the viciousness and power of these tigers of the deep. The shark's teeth— their instruments of death—are the most prized trophy taken from this fish.

Shark jaws command an extremely high price. Jewelry made from shark teeth also brings large sums. The simplest method to acquire the teeth is to catch the shark yourself, remove his dentures, and either sell the entire jaw or make bracelets, necklaces, or earrings from individual teeth with materials acquired at a craft shop. It may be difficult, however, to maintain a constant source of teeth. For this reason, I suggest talking with charter boat captains who catch sharks. Offer to buy a shark's head for a nominal fee. Many sportsmen enjoy catching sharks but have no further use for the fish once they have been landed. If the boat captain knows he can make money merely by cutting off the shark's head and bringing it to you, a dead shark that would have been thrown back into the sea may become a useful product for your business venture. You may find a new market along the coast by showing boat captain that you can take a customer's shark head, cut out the jaw, clean it, dry it, paint it a pearly white, and mount it on a panel suitable for hanging. Some outdoorsmen even may contract with you to take their shark, remove and clean the teeth, and make jewelry for them and their friends.

A dead shark with a good set of teeth is not good to anyone except the person who knows how to use it. Why not be that person and turn a handsome profit?

(17) PREDATOR ORNAMENTS. Although most sportsmen are more familiar with displays made from shark teeth, other "toothy" prizes are

worth investigating as well. The canine teeth of the bobcat, raccoon, fox, coyote, wolf, and bear make excellent pendants, earrings, watch fobs, and key chain ornaments. These trophies are ordinarily thrown away by most taxidermists. By taking a few extra minutes to remove the teeth from many of your specimens, however, you may be able to earn as much as $10.00 to $15.00 for each tooth that otherwise would have been tossed into the garbage.

Wild hog or boar teeth are other potential sources of revenue. Many sportsmen want the original tusks mounted with their boar. Since this requires boiling the jaws, removing the tusks, cutting a plastic jaw set out of the form, and inserting the real teeth, a taxidermist must spend more time implanting original tusks than plastic reproductions. The taxidermist should charge an additional fee for this service.

In cases where the wild sow or boar has less-than-impressive teeth, many hunters will opt for the plastic jaw set. However, the largest part of a boar's tusk is down inside his jaw. So even if your customer chooses the plastic jaw set, you still can recover a long, beautifully curved tooth from the specimen.

Because the hog's tooth is hollow, it often will split with age. The best technique for preventing this from happening is to fill the cavity with hot glue. Next, polish the tooth with jeweler's polish or paint it with a clear lacquer to bring back the luster. Then attach the tooth to a piece of rawhide and flank it on either side with polished deer toenails to make an attractive necklace for a mountain man or Indian costume. As an alternative, you can seal the tusk at the base with a gold or silver cap and attach it to a gold or silver chain to make a neck ornament.

Another lovely piece can be made from the top two teeth of an elk. These beautiful chunks of ivory have been carved and used for ornaments for hundreds of years. The taxidermist who looks at an animal and sees more than the obvious will be the one who increases his income without having to increase the volume of work he receives.

(18) PACK IN HUNDREDS OF DOLLARS AS A MEAT PACKER. Each season, thousands of novice outdoorsmen invade the woodlands and waterways of every state. One of the biggest problems that faces many outdoorsmen—novices and veterans alike—is cleaning game. The thought of plucking a turkey, skinning a deer, dehiding a squirrel, or removing the fur from a rabbit after a hard day afield often discourages hunters. Even after they have removed the hide or feathers, they may not know what to do with the meat.

In some parts of the country, sportsmen charge from $10.00 to $75.00 to cape and skin an animal as well as process and package the meat for the freezer. Some sportsmen will even grind the meat or cut it into serving sizes as specified by the customer.

Although deer are among the most universal big game species in the United States, sportsmen often are ill prepared to deal with the animal after the kill. Therefore, deer are excellent animals to promote in your meat packing business. If you have a large, walk-in cooler, you can offer your customers the advantage of aging their meat as well as skinning and preparing it for the freezer. Once the meat is aged, customers can be offered the choice of having the deer quartered or cut and wrapped for the freezer.

You can even offer to make deer burger or sausage for your customers. The best recipe I have used for making deer burger is 50 percent deer meat, 40 percent beef trimmings, and 10 percent pork trimmings. The beef trimmings are mostly fat but do have some lean in them and can be bought from a butcher shop or meat packing house. You must charge the customer an additional fee for the beef trimmings. All the components should be ground twice and mixed thoroughly.

To prepare deer sausage, use 50 percent deer meat, 40 percent pork trimmings, 10 percent beef trimmings, and the proper amount of Legg's Sausage Seasoning to make the sausage as hot or as mild as your customers want. This recipe cannot be beat for a delicious, flavorful sausage. The spice is available in most stores or write A.C. Legg Packing, P.O. Box 10283, Birmingham, AL 35202 for information.

How many nights have you come in from a duck hunt and been willing to pay fifty cents to $2.00 each for someone to pick, clean, and wrap the ducks you spent all day taking in bad weather? Many hunters find that having someone else care for their game is a real convenience when they are wet and fatigued. These are your potential customers. With a duck picking machine, a meat gambrel, a length of rope, a good tree, a sharp knife, and spare freezer space, you can become the local wild-meat packing house. No extra investments should be made until after your business is paying for itself. You may need an extra refrigerator or, if business is brisk, a walk-in cooler to hold the game if it starts coming in faster than you can care for it. Depending on how ambitiously you plan to attack the market, check with the local health department to see if there are any restrictions or requirements that may necessitate additional equipment.

For this business to prosper, you must realize that you may have to work odd hours and stay up some nights when you ordinarily would spend time with your family or watch television. This is exactly what your customer is paying you to do: to give him that time and properly care for his meat. This service will tie in well with your taxidermy business because much of the same equipment and space can be used for both operations.

(19) WHY NOT SELL A COOKBOOK? The sportsmen who come to

see you are hunters and fishermen. However, more than likely neither they nor their spouses or families are specialists in wildlife preparation. Millions of pounds of good, edible fish and wildlife finds its way to the bellies of hounds rather than to the tables of masters. The sportsman either fails to care for the meat properly in the field, is unable to clean the game correctly, fails to preserve it so as to keep it from drying out and becoming tough, or does not know how to prepare the meat for the table so it is not only wholesome but delicious.

By using your connections in the outdoor field, doing research at the library, and contacting your state's wildlife extension service, fish and wildlife service of the state department of conservation, county extension agent's office, or state university's home economics department, you can glean all the information and recipes you need to compile a cookbook for the outdoorsman. Be sure to concentrate on simple, easy-to-prepare recipes that use readily available ingredients. As a taxidermist you are supposed to be somewhat of an expert on wildlife, so the book will most likely be readily received and eagerly bought.

You can increase the book's appeal and sell more copies by including recipes that have been suggested or tested by your customers and their families. Almost anyone will buy a book that includes his name and some information he has contributed. Not only will he buy one copy, but usually he will purchase copies for all his friends and relatives. Do not overlook this marketing point in your book's preparation. No matter how well your book is written or how good the information is, if no one buys it you will not make any money.

Display the book within easy reach of all who come into your shop. Many hunters will browse, looking at the specimens you have on display and any literature you have on your desk. Make the book easy to see, easy to reach, and hard not to buy. A question like, "Would you like me to add that book in with your mounting charges?" will usually bring an affirmative answer. The size and content of your book or booklet can be tailor made to your area. The selling price should cover all your expenses plus yield a profit.

If the idea of writing a full-sized cookbook seems too big a task and one that may require more time and investment than you are willing to spend, then start with a booklet. A wild-game cooking booklet need not contain more than 8 or 10 pages and can be targeted specifically for your local market. For instance, if much of your business in the winter consists of mounting deerheads, your booklet may include information on how to properly cape, skin, and quarter a deer as well as prepare the venison for the table. This booklet can be either photocopied or printed. Your cost per booklet should be less than $1.00, and you can sell it for $2.00. This same type of booklet can be sold if you are in a place where elk, ducks, moose, or bear are predominant. During the spring and summer, when fish are the primary specimens you receive, you can add another booklet on "How to Freeze, Smoke, or Cook Fish"—especially those fish native to the region you serve.

Each year, as you see more of a particular type of game, you can add a different pamphlet to sell to the customers who bring in various species. Within a year or two you will have written a complete cookbook for the sportsman, while still receiving revenue from the booklets for the specific species. One of the most lucrative commodities sold in this country today is information. The taxidermist who is knowledgeable about the species he mounts should have a vast quantity of this information to sell to his patrons.

(20) THERE IS MONEY IN KILLS AND MISSES. A favorite gift item for many hunters to give rather than to receive is a deer rump mount. These are relatively inexpensive to acquire, easy to do, and highly profitable for the taxidermist. Since many deer are thrown away each year, obtaining a deerskin is not very difficult. If the tail is attached to the skin, you have the makings of a rump mount.

After fleshing the back half of the hide, remove the tailbone by either splitting the tail or holding the skin on the inside of the tail and pulling the bone out. Then take a urethane rump mannequin (available from many of the supply houses listed in the back of this book) and determine how the form fits the skin.

Insert a piece of clothesline wire into the urethane form at what appears to be the butt of the tail. Make the wire long enough so a portion of it can go into the urethane and the protruding part is about the length of the deer's tail from base to tip. Take cotton or excelsior and twine and wrap the wire to build up the tail so it is the same size and dimension as the bone you removed. Next, rub dry preservative thoroughly on the skin and tail. Slip the wire into the tail and pull the skin around the form. Tack the skin to the back of the form and elevate the tail to the desired position. With a strip of waxed cardboard, pin the skin to the form right below the anus where the two hindquarters join. This will ensure that the hide tans correctly to the form. Brush the tail out with the hair flaring from the base, as it does when a deer is frightened. Allow the mount to dry from four to six weeks. Then attach it to a panel and add a nameplate with words like, "Last Deer Shot by Billy Bob," "Sam Jones' Biggest Trophy of the Year," "The Best Deer Seen by John Doe All Season," "The Only Deer Ever Taken by Sam Jones," and so on. With your creative mind you can think up other interesting quotations to go beneath this unusual mount.

Another gag-gift trophy that is more popular each year is made of aluminum beer cans and soft drink containers. These cans or bottles are glued to panels with nameplates that read, for example, "One of 1000 Killed by James Black," "The Only Thing Bill Jones Killed during Hunting Season," "The Biggest Thing Fred Smith Ever Killed," and so on.

(21) THE INDIANS ARE BACK. In most areas of the country, Indian lore and crafts are being revived. Since the Indians derived their living from the use of animals, the alert taxidermist can seek out these individuals and groups and supply them with many would-be throwaway items such as extra skins, deer feet, deer toenails, bird feathers, and so on. One of the magazines particularly interested in these types of items is *Indian Trader,* Box 867, Gallup, NM 87301. Also check with your state historical society and state bureau of publicity and information for others who may be interested in these articles. Be sure to find out if there are local Indian groups in your area or state. Write to these groups to find out when and if they have powwows or arts and crafts days and if they have a tribal paper where you can advertise your items. By talking with members of local tribes you may be able to determine some of their needs and fill them.

(22) THE CLICK IS THE TRICK. You let hundreds of dollars escape your grasp each day in the taxidermy business without realizing it. The reason customers come to your studio is to have their trophies mounted as remembrances of hunting or fishing trips. Often, a sportsman is so excited about his trophy and so intent on getting it to you before it spoils that he forgets to take a good picture of his prize.

Keep a 35 mm camera, loaded with professional-quality film, and a flash attachment handy so you can take a picture of a customer and his trophy prior to mounting. You can sell an 8" x 10" color picture (which will cost you no more than $2.00 to $3.50) to your customer for $8.00 to $10.00. Add a charge for framing. Always keep samples of your work in frames in your exhibit room and display a three-ring binder with plastic pages full of photos on your desk at all times. Becoming known for your photography may lead to your taking pictures of horses, dogs, and so on during your off season. Be sure to use a rubber stamp to imprint "Photo by," followed by your name, address, and telephone number, on the backs of the pictures.

Another good way to use your camera—not only to make extra money but also to advertise your business—is to send a picture of your customer with his trophy to a local newspaper or magazine. Give the name of the person who took the trophy, where and when he took it, and an accompanying credit such as "Photo Furnished by John Phillips'

Even if this hunter is going to have the deer's head mounted, it'll be several months before he can get it home. In the meantime, a quality photo can be his personal memento of the day, and you can be the one to set it up—and sell it for an extra money-maker on the project.

Taxidermy Studio." This little extra service for your customers will draw you more business because:

1. People seeing the photo will also read the name of your business,

2. Some folks will bring you specimens to mount in hopes of getting their photos in a newspaper or magazine, and

3. Editors who see the quality of your photos may call on you to do some outdoor photography for their publications.

Often, by accompanying the outdoor editor of your local newspaper on hunting and fishing trips and shooting the photos for him, you may be able to work into a position to fill your extra time during the off-season. Taking good outdoor photos can be a lucrative business for the taxidermist who learns how to use a camera.

Two excellent reference books for outdoor photographers are *Hunting with a Camera* by Erwin A. Bauer and *The Outdoor Photographer's Handbook* by Kenn Oberrecht. Both are published by Winchester Press. C. Boyd Pfeiffer's *Field Guide to Outdoor Photography* is also a good source for learning about making pictures in the outdoors.

One summer, when I had more time than money, I began to look for different aspects of the outdoor field to turn into income. I knew many quail hunters and a shooting preserve operator. The operator of the shooting preserve also trained bird dogs for sportsmen. Working with the operator, I took color photos of each bird dog he was training. We brought each dog up to a pen-raised bird. Then, when the pointer or setter locked into pointing position, I took several color photos. I had small color proofs made of each dog and sent them to the owners, stating that they could keep the proofs for $2.00 each, have 8" x 10" prints made for $9.00 each, or purchase an 8" x 10" color photo in a beautiful wood grain frame with nonglare glass for $15.95 plus $1.25 postage and handling. Being a dog photographer really paid off well during the off-season and put me into contact with other outdoorsmen who later brought me taxidermy work.

(23) OTHER PROFESSIONALS CAN AID YOUR PROFESSION. The best friend a taxidermist can make is an interior decorator. In planning and designing more livable homes for people, some decorators have adopted the idea of bringing the outdoors indoors to produce more natural surroundings. By purchasing specimens from game ranches, shooting preserves, and tanneries, an enterprising taxidermist may discover a market that has been waiting for him to appear. You need to remember that the interior decorator has a particular image or mood he is trying to project with your specimens, so let him tell you what he wants. Even if his needs are a problem, learn to solve them.

One day a short, immaculately dressed man came into our shop and asked, "Do you have any skins for sale?" As I looked over my desk, I wondered what this fellow might want with animal skins.

By combining your talents with those of other professionals, you can broaden the scope of your services. A floral arrangement with this hen pheasant mount is an example.

"Yes, sir, I sure do," I said as I showed him beaver-, coon-, and deerskins. The man, who was an interior decorator, chose a couple of prime beaver pelts from which to make pillows for the couch of a wealthy client. Before he left, he also had purchased several mounted specimens and had ordered a deer-foot coat rack. Our association with this decorator has been very beneficial over the past few years. He usually buys almost everything we have to sell.

Large furniture stores often employ one or more interior decorators on their staffs. When choosing furniture and art for their homes, most clients want to see the pieces in a grouping. For this reason, showrooms are set up to resemble actual dining rooms, bedrooms, dens, and so on. The taxidermist who is trying to create a new market for his mounted specimens should browse through furniture showrooms to determine which specimens would look best in which settings. By offering the interior decorator mounted specimens to display with a particular groupings, you may sell more specimens than you would have by displaying them individually. When the store owner and his personnel realize that you are not only trying to sell your wares (from which they can make a profit) but are actually trying to help them sell furniture and home decorations, they may become more interested in working with you. Remember that when you sell a specimen through a decorator or a furniture store, they must also make a profit for displaying your craft. For this reason, you may have to charge more for specimens sold in showrooms than those sold in your shop.

Where not restricted by law, trappers can provide you with lovely pelts that you can mount and sell to your customers. Remember that you're just not selling to those sportsmen who bring in a bird, deer, or other animal, but also to those folks who want to decorate their homes with wildlife art.

Some excellent critters for the home furnishings market are game-ranch pheasants, game-farm mallard ducks, chukar quail, or bobwhite quail—all mounted in habitat scenes with dried flowers, color coordinated to complement the showroom furniture. And some taxidermists have discovered that combining their craft with that of a furniture maker can help both artists make a handsome profit. Hardwood desks with mounted quail scenes encased in glass, or glass coffee tables and end tables with outdoor scenes featuring quail, ducks, or other mounted specimens, have also become popular. You may have several other ideas for furniture that feature mounted specimens to give a new dimension to the furniture maker's art.

(24) FROM QUAIL HEADS TO COWBOY HATS. Another business venture that proved lucrative for me over a two-year period developed quite unexpectedly. I had just come in from a hunting trip when my wife, Denise, greeted me with a strange question.

"Do we mount quail heads?" she asked.

"Sure, we mount quail heads, quail feet, quail tails, all or any part of a quail that someone wants mounted," I answered as I grinned.

"Well, this fellow called and wanted to know how much you charged to mount quail heads," she said. "I told him I didn't know, but that you would call him when you got back to town. I don't know what he is going to do with the quail heads, but you should call and talk to him."

The following morning I called the man and quoted a price of $5.00 per head with a minimum of 25 heads. Then he wanted a price on mounting the quail heads with the breasts still attached. I bid $15.00.

"Then how much will you charge to preserve the wings?" he asked.

"$1.00 a pair," I replied.

Finally, when my curiosity could wait no longer to be satisfied, I inquired, "What are you going to do with these when I get them mounted?"

"I'll put backings on them and sell them to go on cowboy hats," he said.

I thought to myself, "If he can sell the quail heads, I can mount them. There may be some money in this for both of us."

During the next two years we mounted thousands of quail heads, wings, breasts, and tails. Many an urban cowboy went to the local nightclubs with one of my specimens atop his stetson. The quail heads became such a fad that even construction workers had them glued to their hard hats. I have to admit my taxidermy work created a lot of attention resting atop someone's head.

Then, one day, my partner came in and said, "One of the country and western stars on tv has a muskrat head mounted on top of his cowboy hat. Can we do something like that?"

"Oh, we can beat that," I said. "We can customize a hat for any occasion. Bring me a hat tomorrow. Within two weeks I will show you something that will excite you."

I went to my freezer and found a gray squirrel I had taken during the past season, I cut the squirrel in half, preserved the hide and head, and stuffed the body and arms with cotton. In the back of the front half of the squirrel I inserted a piece of urethane to use to pin the skin to and as a base to attach my creation to the hat. The rear half of the squirrel was shortened so that just the legs and tail were mounted. The tail was supported by a piece of wire and swept to the top of the hat, then bent down like a question mark. The feet stood on the hat's brim as if poised to jump. The front half was mounted to make it appear as though the squirrel was holding on by reaching its paws over the front of the brim. The ears were erect. The hat was unusual. Anyone seeing it from the side might think that the squirrel had run right through the crown. The customer who bought the hat now sported a stetson that would make even the most famous country and western star turn green with envy.

Most often the sportsman must provide the specimen for mounting animals and ducks in unusual positions. However, game farm animals such as ducks, quail, pheasants, and chukars can be legally purchased and mounted for resale in most states. A good magazine offering information on game farms and ranches from which you can buy specimens is *Wildlife Harvest*, Rt. 1, Box 28, Goose Lake, IA 52750. The cost is $1.25 per issue.

(25) THE MOST RESOURCEFUL TAXIDERMIST I'VE EVER MET.
Several years ago, when our country was going through a recession and money became tight, my brother, Archie, and I began to worry about the future of our businesses. While we were discussing the problem of hard times, the name of Shelby Butts came up.

Butts had been in taxidermy for 50 years—even through the Great Depression of the 1930s. We felt that with his knowledge and experience he could enlighten us as to what we might expect in our business if money got tight or the country went through another depression.

"There's one thing you boys apparently do not understand," the grizzled man told us. "And this is the key to all business. People will buy what they want and owe for what they need."

The magnitude of this statement is the pillow upon which the taxidermy profession rests. Butts continued:

> During the Depression, if a man caught a trophy bass, killed a big buck, or took a beautiful specimen of any kind, he would want it mounted. To get the

The array of devices available today make work like this appear crude. Here the taxidermist used a skull, a bit of clay, and a piece of cedar. You can see the work that went into getting the form ready before it was wrapped and formed for the final product. It's easier these days with pre-formed shapes.

money to do it he would beg, borrow, steal, or barter. I remember one man for whom I mounted a deer head. When it was time for the animal to be picked up, the man explained that he had no money but that if I would bring my truck up into the country where he lived, he would load me up with meat and vegetables. I agreed and on the appointed Saturday went to work to meet the man. I was given smoked pork, canned beef, bacon, ham, and a load of vegetables put up in jars. It took my family two years to eat all that food for which we traded that one deer mount.

Prices in the 1930s were a lot different than they are now. We charged $15.00 for mounting a deer head, $3.00 for tanning the hide, and $5.00 for mounting a fish. I also made ceramic figurines and painted them and even carved a few tombstones. But during the Depression I had more cash money than anyone in my county. There has always been and always will be a good living in taxidermy for the man who is willing to work.

Butts was resourceful in every way. He went into the woods with a crosscut saw, cut trees down, split them into lumber, dried the wood in a kiln he had made, planed the boards by hand, glued the pieces together, and cut out and finished his own panels. He wrapped his own forms out of string and excelsior. He never wasted anything.

Butts built his reputation as a taxidermist by going to every hunting club in his area and offering to skin and cape—for free—all the deer killed by the members. Butts realized that the key to the taxidermy business is not only quality work but also the personality of the taxidermist. He was a friend to every hunter and fisherman within several counties of his business. If they had a problem, a need, or a question, if they sought advice or information, Butts was the man they called. He stayed up to date on the game laws and treated his customers like friends instead of clients. For this reason, his business grew and prospered.

Sometimes the most overlooked ingredient in a successful business is the customer-proprietor relationship. Every customer who leaves your studio should come in as a client and go out as a friend. Then you have a friend recommending you to his friends instead of a customer for whom you perform a service and may never see again. Butts' resourcefulness was not only demonstrated in his ability to build a successful business, but also in his talent to continue to serve the clients in his area and build friendships.

One of the best pieces of business advice and the best tip this book can give you is found in one of the oldest chronicles of successful business, the Bible. Matt. 20:26-27 states, "But whosoever will be great among you, let him be a minister, And whosoever will be chief among you, let him be a servant." It is that servant attitude and willingness to meet needs that generates income.

If a sportsman had a need, Shelby Butts could find some way to fill it. In so doing, he was able to earn more than just a living for his family and himself. Being resourceful is the key to not only success but also longevity in our chosen profession.

(26) DO THE TOUGHIES. Thousands of dollars are lost each year by taxidermists because they lack resourcefulness and creativity or are just too lazy to attempt something they have never done before. Some taxidermists turn down work because it will cause them additional problems or worry not usually associated with the specimens they customarily mount. But the motto of our studio is "Problems are our business." We accept all the odd jobs, the tedious and time-consuming jobs other taxidermists turn away. We charge for the extra problems, however, to compensate for the additional time required to do these difficult specimens. If a way exists to mount a specimen, we try to find it. We believe our philosophy of solving problems adds 30 percent more work to our studio each year.

A classic example of this problem-solving philosophy involves a telephone call we received a couple of years ago.

"Mr. Phillips, can you hang a water buffalo?" the caller asked. Thinking at first that this was a crank call, I assured the lady we could hang anything that could be legally hung in the state.

She chuckled and explained, "No, you don't understand. My boss is the head of his department here at the hospital. He's gone on vacation. His last instructions to me were, 'I want that water buffalo on the wall in my office before I come back. I don't care what you have to do to get him there, but I want him hanging when I walk back in the door.' Our maintenance men have tried and haven't come up with a way to put the animal in the office. I was promised that if anyone could do the job it would be you. Can you do it?"

With that kind of challenge, I immediately told her we could solve her problem, but that the fee for me to leave my studio, bring an assistant and tools to the hospital, and hang the water buffalo that very day would be $100.00.

"Price isn't the problem," she commented. "Hanging the buffalo is the problem." With that understanding, I told her we were on our way. Because of the location of the hospital, structure of the building, and design of the room, it took us about two hours to get to the hospital and hang the buffalo, but the job was done to everyone's satisfaction. The check was made out and we were paid. A price of $50.00 per hour may seem exorbitant, but when you include travel time and time away from the studio, the price is really fair.

A few nights ago my tv went on the blink so I called a service man. He looked at my set, walked behind it, pushed the reset button, and it started working. He charged me $25.00.

"Outrageously high!" you may think. But not really, because the man knew which button to punch. The same idea applies to taxidermists. If you can solve a problem no one else can, then the pay for doing that job should reflect your expertise.

(27) THE TAXIDERMIST AS AN OUTDOOR COMMUNICATOR. "The twentieth century will be the age of the specialist," we were told in our formative years.

"Highly skilled and well-trained professionals will be the leaders of the day," our teachers said, and they were right to a degree. However, most of us have found money in taxidermy only through developing various skills in a wide range of fields. An enterprising craftsman will learn related skills in the outdoor field to fall back on when the fish and animals do not arrive in sufficient volume to pay the rent or provide sufficient personal income.

I was made keenly aware of this law some years ago. After I finished college, my taxidermy business began to grow each year. We were seeing a 25 to 40 percent annual increase in the volume of work. From all appearances we would have an extremely large business with many employees in a short period of time. We bought a building, built forms, and enlarged our operation in an effort to prepare for an ever-expanding business. At the peak of our growth, however, a recession in our area resulted in fewer people having specimens mounted and more people seeking part-time work as taxidermists. Any time people are laid off from work or wind up with more time than money, there is usually a surge of new taxidermists. To compound the problem even more, the deer kill in our region was less than it had been in previous years.

The net result of all these problems was that the volume of our taxidermy business was 50 percent less than it had been in previous years. Having bought supplies, hired employees, and purchased equipment in expectation of a 25 percent growth factor for the year, my annual income was 75 percent less than anticipated and at least 50 percent less than the previous year. The future looked very bleak, at best. With bills beginning to mount, I looked for alternatives to conventional taxidermy.

Any taxidermist who has been in the trade for at least five years should have developed contacts who know how to fish and hunt better than many other sportsmen. He also should have good relationships with conservation officials and fishing and wildlife clubs in his region. These people, I realized, were sources I could use to glean information that would benefit thousands of other outdoorsmen in my state. If I could communicate the information and knowledge that these people had to the masses, surely I would be able to make money and work my way out of the financial dilemma. Since desperation seems to make me think quickly, I studied the possibilities of writing outdoor columns and broadcasting an outdoor program on the radio. I wrote several hundred letters of inquiry and made two or three dozen telephone calls to find out that no one was interested in either the radio program or the newspaper column. I still felt, however, that the outdoor information I collected from other sportsmen would eventually pay off if I persevered.

Newspapers

The technique that finally worked for me was to submit several sample outdoor columns to newspapers. These samples were typed, double spaced, on 8-1/2" x 11" plain white paper, then photocopied. The articles were primarily about other people and what they did to take game or catch fish. A column about oneself is not as effective and may lack enough information to satisfy the reader. A better approach for an upbeat, informative column is to write about a hunter who consistently takes a deer or two every season, or a noted fisherman in the area. Other ideas may include interviewing the local conservation officer about new game laws or talking with a wildlife biologist about habitat changes and the best places to look for game in a given area. Hundreds of other experts will be of interest to your readers as well. As you interview and write about these individuals, they can help convince your editor to pay you a salary.

You may start off by offering these weekly columns free of charge to a newspaper that does not have an outdoor section. After your column runs for two or three weeks, talk with the editor about some type of pay for your work. By following this plan, within six months I was able to syndicate a weekly column in 27 newspapers in my state. Each newspaper received the same column, and each paid the same amount. However, the revenue received from writing newspaper columns was not sufficient to make up the financial deficit from my taxidermy business.

Radio

The next step was to venture into the radio industry. Because of the number of sportsmen who come through a taxidermy shop daily, most taxidermists have the opportunity to interview hundreds of outdoorsmen each year. Each hunter or angler has an interesting story, a different technique, or a unique or often-overlooked way to take fish and wildlife. By keeping a tape recorder handy, the taxidermist can get a week's worth of outstanding radio programs without leaving his office. Although he has the material for radio shows on his cassette tape recorder, however, he will not generate income unless he can find a radio station that is willing to air his program.

One method that worked well for me was to play the demonstration tape for a radio station manager. If he liked the program, I offered to help sell the advertising that would pay not only for the air time but for my fee as well. After selling my program to the first radio station, I succeeded in selling the same program to 23 other stations throughout the state.

Often we taxidermists look at the pure dollar value of the items our customers bring in for us to mount. I have found that many times customers have information, experiences, and stories equal to or greater than the amount of profit that can be made by mounting their specimens. Each customer brings two potential sources of profit to the taxidermist: the specimen he carries in his hands and the information he has in his head. The specimen's profit is easy to see, but the sportsman's knowledge is invisible. Yet, by probing, you may uncover the essentials for a greater profit. Most people enjoy seeing their names and the information they have given you in print. It satisfies their egos and is something they can brag about to their friends and family.

The difference between a man who can take a deer head, mount it, and turn it into a profit and the man who sees the deer head, knows there is a profit in it, but never attempts to mount the specimen is equivalent to the taxidermist who hears a new and better way to hunt or fish, an exciting adventure story, or a tip on how to make outdoor living more fun and does not turn that useful knowledge into dollars.

Television

Several years ago my brother, Archie, was asked to be the moderator of a tv program on the outdoors. Archie had no training in public speaking, much less in broadcasting. However, he was well versed in all aspects of hunting and fishing because of his many years in the taxidermy profession. He also knew sportsmen around the state who had varying and interesting outdoor skills. Boat dock operators, hunting club presidents, game wardens, wildlife biologists, and wildlife researchers were all only a telephone call away. Archie quickly learned to operate a 16 mm movie camera. In less time than it takes to give an argument for why he could not be an outdoor broadcaster, he was one. His tv program also contained an ad for his taxidermy business. In effect, he was advertising his taxidermy business while drawing revenue from his tv program.

Sometimes the door of opportunity fails to swing open because we are afraid to grab the handle and pull. There may be a tv station in your area that does not now have a program on the outdoors and may never have one until somebody goes to them with the idea of starting such a show. The reason television stations air programs is to generate revenue from sponsors to pay salaries and upkeep and create a profit. Even though you may be very knowledgeable and personable and have vast experience in the outdoor field, no station manager will air your program unless it generates revenue. The likelihood of selling a show without sponsorship is extremely slim. To provide the advertising you need for your taxidermy business, the income you desire to pay your bills, and the profit margin the tv station must realize before it consents to make you an airway star, somebody must sell the advertising time. The surest way to secure your future is for you to sell the advertising. Then you can go to the station manager with not only a quality program idea but a list of businesses that have agreed to sponsor your program for 13 weeks to six months. Once again, your customers will point you in the direction of the advertisers who will be willing to pay the fee to air your information. However, you will have to call on the potential advertisers and sell them on the idea that your tv program will help bolster their businesses.

Magazines

Many taxidermists view magazine writers as an elitist group of photojournalists. However, they are merely people with information to sell, much like the taxidermist. A writer without a story is not a writer but an unemployed pencil pusher.

There are two ways for a taxidermist to venture into the magazine market:

1. You can provide the magazine writer with a source of stories and information he can turn into articles. Most writers will be more than happy to mention the taxidermist who puts them onto a story or supplies them with the information they need to write a story.
2. If you are a braver soul, you can write your own magazine articles. However, some cautions should be kept in mind. If you plan to write magazine articles about the taxidermy trade or some of the customers who frequent your office, remember that your submissions need to be typed double-spaced on 20-pound bond paper. They should also be grammatically correct and in magazine format.

Several sources can help you produce a satisfactory manuscript. The simplest method is to contact an English teacher or English major and have them edit your work for accuracy and clarity. *Writer's Market,* a book published yearly and available at almost all bookstores and libraries, gives guidelines for proper manuscript preparation and submission to magazines. If you cannot locate a copy of this book, write to *Writer's Market,* Writer's Digest Books, 9933 Alliance Rd., Cincinnati, OH 45242.

To ensure a good chance that your work will be published, include a selection of both black-and-white and color photos with your article. The black-and-white pictures must be glossy 8" x 10"s with high contrast and your color submissions should be Kodachrome 64 slides. These photos should illustrate all aspects of the article you have written.

The best place to break into the magazine market as a taxidermy journalist is to submit articles to the trade magazines like *Taxidermy Review, American Taxidermist,* and *Modern Taxidermy.* These maga-

---

zines, whose addresses are listed in the back of this book, always are eager for information about the taxidermy trade and new insights into how to make business more profitable.

Writing is learned. To learn to write, you must write. Whether you ever sell the words or not is irrelevant. As a weightlifter lifts hundreds of thousands of pounds to develop his muscles and prepare his body and mind for competition, so must the taxidermist work to develop his writing skills. Read all the outdoor magazines, booklets, and pamphlets you can—not necessarily for what they say, but for the way they say it. Then, if you plan to get serious about your writing, write a minimum of 500 words a day about any subject.

General Ideas On How a Taxidermist Can Be An Outdoor Writer

1. A writer must first be a reporter.
   a. Learn to write about "who, where, when, why, and caught on or shot with what."
   b. Learn where to find sources of information—sportsmen who come into your shop, marinas, conservation officers, fish camps, and so on.
   c. Don't always write about your friends.
   d. Mention yourself as little as possible. Once you have established yourself as a reporter, your readership will know you from your byline.
   e. Write what the readers want to read, not what you want to write.
   f. Don't let your writing become a self-edifying ego trip, but rather a tool for promoting the outdoor experience and hunting and fishing in your area.
2. Take samples of three of the best stories you have written—with good 8″ x 10″ black-and-white, glossy photos—to the editor of the newspaper for whom you would like to write a column. Also include a copy of your personal biography to establish your credentials.
3. Always present your column to the managing editor of the paper first. If he wants to send you to the sports editor, he will. Always start at the top. If you begin with the sports editor, you may not have the opportunity to present your column to the person who can make the decision and write you a check.
4. Weekly or biweekly newspapers are usually the best places to start. Because they have low budgets, most small newspapers are not able to afford a full-time outdoor writer. But they may be willing to pay $3.00 to $10.00 for each weekly column and more for pictures.
5. Getting your material in print should be your primary concern, since it boosts your self-image. If your work is in print, someone will read it and that someone may be a potential customer.

6. In several columns each year, give instructions on caring for trophies in the field, skinning for the trophy mount, and preparing wild-game recipes. These articles will give you credibility and establish you as a reputable taxidermist in the minds of your readers.

7. A newspaper column may be the cheapest advertising for which you ever traded.

Tips and Hints For Writing Articles

1. Know what you're writing about. Research your subject. Get specific. Do your homework before you ever touch the typewriter keys.

2. Make sure you know what writing is about. Most beginning authors foolishly think their work is good or bad because of style. But the real question is whether or not the author has anything worthwhile or interesting to communicate. Ideas and emotions are what writing and editing are really all about—not words, punctuation, syntax, grammar, or style. To be an effective writer, get a pure idea out of your head or a pure emotion out of your heart and put that idea or emotion into the head or the heart of your reader. According to Gene Hill, one of the nation's top outdoor writers, "If you can talk it and explain it, then you can write it. But you will have to stop, listen to your words as you say them, and then write them. Progress step by step."

3. Remember that stories and even "how-to" articles have a beginning, middle, and end. Organize your piece. Start it off strong, let it lead your reader naturally and logically through all the information you have to present, and give it a sensible and satisfying reason to end. Remember that the "great circle" method of organizing an article— in which the reader is first confronted with a problem, then given a solution, and finally led back past a variation of the opening thought—is hard to beat.

4. Get right into your article. Do not apologize. Do not explain. And do not pass the time of day. Just plunge right in after setting the stage in a single opening paragraph.

5. A time sequence is hard to beat when you are organizing a "how-to" article. Break your total lump of information down into bite-sized pieces. Then put your arm around the reader's shoulders and spoon feed that nourishment starting with the appetizer and proceeding through the soup and salad to the main course and closing with the dessert. Stop after writing each paragraph and ask yourself if it is clear. Then rewrite if necessary.

6. Have a regard for flow. Maybe we all spend too much time being

brainwashed by the shortcuts of television. But when a writer knocks off all the transitional words and phrases, the copy becomes much harder and more jolting to read even though it is shortened and streamlined. Use transitional words and phrases such as *still, on the other hand, however, although, of course, remember, first, next, then, last, finally, once again,* and so on.

7. Always strive to write with absolute clarity. Bear in mind constantly that the English language is a very imperfect carrier of ideas and emotions.

8. Leave nothing to chance in a "how-to" article. Do not abbreviate words. If you give your reader an unfamiliar term, include a definition. Explain right then what you mean. Clarify, clarify.

9. Beware of clipped thoughts. Say what you mean and say it completely.

10. Use synonyms for main nouns. "Poles, poles, poles," is never as interesting as "poles, branches, sticks, rods, and so on." Use synonyms to refer to the main characters in your articles, but remember that every paragraph of every article should be treated as a little story all its own. Identify the main character in no uncertain terms at the beginning of the paragraph and then and only then think about using a pronoun to refer to that character.

11. Use synonyms for main verbs. People do not just walk. They also trudge, skip, stagger, bounce, pace, proceed, advance, and so on.

12. Use synonyms for other parts of speech. Depending on the effect you are after, *hard, stiff, rigid, solid, dense, compact,* and several other words can be substituted for the adjective *firm.* Purchase a college-level dictionary, *Roget's Thesaurus,* and *The Synonym Finder* by U.I. Rodale and staff, which is available from Rodale Books, Inc., Emmaus, PA 18049.

13. Vary everything about your sentences: length, structure, meter, and so on. Active-voice verbs, however, should outnumber passive-voice sentences by about 4000 to one. The active sentences move an article with more authority, drive, and command. "The wind slammed the gate shut" is active. "The gate was slammed shut by the wind" is passive.

14. If you can avoid it, do not use the same word two different ways in the same sentence or paragraph.

15. Learn to use punctuation to add clarity, sparkle, and impact to your writing. Commas are probably the most overworked punctuation in the English language. Parentheses, dashes, and quotations are underused, as are underlines and ellipses.

16. Have a regard for the sequential nature of the English language. "Go throw the horse over the fence some hay," may make good

sense to a Pennsylvania Dutchman but not to most readers of English. Legally declaring a company bankrupt is not necessarily the same as declaring that firm legally bankrupt.

17. "How-to" articles are usually more exciting when written in the present tense. In general, whenever you can tell someone how to do something *right now,* you are ahead of the game.

18. Use subheads when you write an article, if the editor does not mind. Sometimes writers forget that sections of an article are almost always made up of paragraphs plus paragraphs. The reader can follow the train of thought if you erect special signposts between those sections.

19. Use sidebars. Sidebars are miniarticles that completely explain some fact, idea, or body of knowledge that is highly supportive of— but not necessarily essential to—the main article. Sidebars have their own heads and are usually boxed or otherwise set off in some way from the main articles they accompany. Do you have some information that you just cannot seem to fit into the smooth flow of your piece? Make it into a sidebar.

20. Watch your language.

21. Know the limitations of the written word. Sometimes a sketch, drawing, or photograph can transmit an idea or an emotion much better and with much greater impact than can copy.

22. Write bright. Make your article interesting.

How To Take Photographs

1. Remember: There are long, medium, and close-up shots. Send the editor some of each.

2. Pose your pictures, but make them look unposed. Think before you snap that shutter.

3. Look past your subject before you squeeze the button. Distracting, cluttered backgrounds and trees "growing" out of someone's head ruin otherwise good photographs more often than anything else.

4. Focus the camera sharply on your main subject. A smaller lens opening, such as f/16, admits less light so a longer exposure is necessary than with a larger lens opening, such as f/4. But the smaller opening will increase the exposure's depth of field, thereby making focus less critical.

5. Always shoot at least twice as much film as you think you need to shoot. People blink, scratch, and do all sorts of unnoticed things that goof up otherwise good photos. Allow for that while you are shooting.

6. Hold that camera still when you mash the button.

1. Purchase a copy of *Photographer's Market* for the current year from your local bookstore or by writing Writer's Digest Books, 9933 Alliance Rd., Cincinnati, OH 45242.
2. Purchase a copy of *Writer's Market* for the current year from your local bookstore or by writing Writer's Digest Books, 9933 Alliance Rd., Cincinnati, OH 45242.
3. Get a subscription to *Writer's Digest,* 9933 Alliance Rd., Cincinnati, OH 45242, which is a monthly magazine with tips on how to write and the markets available.

Public Speaking and Teaching

A taxidermist who not only studies his trade but also learns all he can about the specimens he mounts is a walking encyclopedia of information on the outdoors. His ability to turn this knowledge into dollars is directly related to what opportunities he finds to communicate that information. Often, finding a program for a civic group can be a nightmare, especially in a small town. Although most taxidermists are not trained speakers, we all should have something to say. The taxidermist should be one of the most informed people in town on conservation issues, hunting and fishing tactics, and many other related skills that make interesting programs. By speaking to these groups, showing slides, and bringing mounted specimens to meetings, you can advertise your business and increase your credibility in the outdoor field.

Schools and seminars dealing with the outdoors have undergone a revival. The big bass boom of the mid-1970s has brought about a whole new generation of better-informed, better-educated sportsmen who search out and pay for knowledge that will help them catch more fish. This quest for information also has spilled over into the hunting market in a way that can be profitable for the taxidermist. In days gone by, magazines were full of stories of hair-raising outdoor adventures and exciting fishing trips in faraway places. However, if you look at the magazine racks today you will see that the primary stories they carry are packed with ideas on how to hunt better or new techniques to enlarge the number and size of fish a sportsman takes.

This kind of information pours into the taxidermist's shop each day. With the increase in noncredit adult education programs offered by most colleges and universities, the taxidermist may find part-time employment by developing courses in hunting, fishing, and outdoor-related skills. Either he or an expert in the field can teach the course.

While noncredit college courses in area schools are good sources of revenue for the taxidermist, so are courses taught in bow-hunting schools, deer-hunting schools, wing-shooting schools, fly-casting schools, and so on. Even if the taxidermist cannot teach all the major skills involved, he can teach related skills.

In a deer-hunting school the taxidermist may use diagrams of the anatomy of the deer and/or a whole mounted deer to teach how to make a one-shot kill. He can show the students where to aim from different directions to down the deer with one shot. The mounted deer can be set up in different parts of a wooded lot to instruct the students what to look for as well as when to hold their shots and wait for the deer to move into a clearing so an accurate, well-placed bullet will bring it down instantly.

A taxidermist also may teach how to prepare the trophy for mounting. Skinning, caping, and quartering can be taught separately or as one course. Blood trailing and tracking are skills that most taxidermists should have. By showing the students the length and color of the hair on a tanned deerskin, the taxidermist can teach how to read the hair that may have fallen when the bullet entered the animal to help determine where the shot was placed. Laying out a blood trail by using a mixture of glycerine (which can be purchased at any drugstore) and food coloring, the taxidermist can demonstrate to students how to read a blood trail and some of the things to look for when tracking a wounded animal.

In a wing-shooting school the taxidermist/sportsman can show how to properly prepare and care for specimens in the field. He may give cooking demonstrations to illustrate how to prepare birds for the table. In an angling school he may give fishermen insights as to the best areas to fish, what baits to use, and how to fish particular types of structure within their region. The taxidermist knows from his clients where the most big fish are coming from, what they are being caught on, and the method used to take them. Always include instructions on how to care for the trophy in the field and how to properly clean fish and provide several good recipes.

By doing some research, an instructor in a turkey-hunting school can inform his students on where to find turkeys, the history of the turkeys in their region, hunting techniques that have been employed to bag big gobblers, how to properly care for the birds in the field, and the different options the sportsman has when he wants to have his turkey mounted.

As you can see, endless opportunities are available to the taxidermist who realizes the volume of knowledge he has and is interested in sharing that information. If you are unable, or feel that you are unable, to speak before a group, spend some time and money on a public speaking course. Also learn to take good slides you can show when you lecture. There is nothing more boring than sitting for hours listening to someone talk without some visual stimuli. So consider carefully what type of visual aids you can use to excite and educate your students.

One source of visual aids vastly overlooked by most outdoor instructors are the numerous films available in the hunting and fishing industry. In many cases these films are available free of charge or at a very low price and are packed full of helpful information that will enable you to teach a better outdoor program. Some good sources to consult on outdoor films are the American Fishing Tackle Manufacturers Association, 2625 Clearbrook Dr., Arlington Heights, IL 60005; the Bass Anglers Sportsman's Society (BASS), 1 Bell Rd., P.O. Box 17900, Montgomery, AL 36141; the National Rifle Association, 1600 Rhode Island Ave., NW Washington, DC 20036; and the National Shooting Sports Foundation, P.O. Box 1075, Riverside, CT 06878. Also check with your local department of conservation, which may have films and also a lot of handout information that will be of vital interest to your students.

An outdoor communicator should be the best customer at his local library's reference department. The librarians' responsibility is to help you find whatever information you may need. These specialists are well trained. Even if they do not have the information available, they will know where to begin looking for it.

An excellent book that will help you to communicate outdoor skills is *Communicating the Outdoor Experience,* which is the Outdoor Writers Association of America (OWAA) manual. Write to the association at 3101 W. Peoria Ave., Suite A-207, Phoenix, AR 85029.

A new field has opened up in the past three or four years for the accomplished taxidermist who can teach. State chapters have been formed by the National Taxidermist Association (NTA). Master taxidermists now train other taxidermists in their particular areas of expertise. You may be accomplished in bird mounting, small animal taxidermy, fish painting, and so on, and taxidermists in other locations may be willing to pay your expenses—plus a fee—for you to visit and teach them your skills. There also may be people interested in taxidermy who would be willing to pay a fee for you to teach them specialty areas in the trade or general taxidermy skills. One of the best methods you can use to become more informed about the trade and learn new skills is to join the NTA.

So whether you communicate via newspapers, radio, television, magazines, public speaking, teaching, or all of these channels, the field is wide open to the taxidermist willing to use the information he has and perfect the skills he needs.

(28) THE NTA AND PROFESSIONAL JOURNALS WILL BROADEN YOUR HORIZONS AND EXPAND YOUR BANK ACCOUNT. The NTA's conference held each year is a must for all serious-minded artists.

At the convention you will learn new methods of mounting and how to handle hard-to-mount specimens, see new products, and become acquainted with taxidermists from all over the world. The exchange of ideas and information you receive at the convention will become a springboard for additional revenue in your profession. If you want to make more money in taxidermy, save your money for the convention and go with an open mind ready to learn. The more you learn, the more information you will have to sell and the more money you will make in taxidermy.

Professional taxidermy journals are an asset to every taxidermist. *Modern Taxidermy*, Greenfield Center, NY 12833, *Taxidermy Review*, 747 Santa Fe Dr., Denver, CO 80204, *American Taxidermist*, P.O. Box 11186, Albuquerque, NM 87192, and *Taxidermy Today*, 119 Gadsden St., Chester, SC 29706 contain articles about innovations, equipment, supplies, and materials that will add dollars to your taxidermy business. You can learn mounting techniques, be apprised of methods used to win national competitions, and learn procedures that will speed up the time required to mount a specimen.

Joseph Bruchac, a veteran taxidermist who has been involved in the trade for many years, publishes *Modern Taxidermy*, which is full of tips, crafts, and suggestions that will make you money. Bruchac and the writers of the magazine also keep you informed on the latest laws as they affect taxidermy and the taxidermist. Some of the best craftsmen in our trade demonstrate the special things they do to their mounts that make them more lifelike and will improve the quality of your work.

Taxidermy Review's editor-in-chief is Joe Kish, another longtime taxidermist. This magazine specializes in practical, "how-to" instructions for sculpting and modeling that will give your specimens more of a museum quality and add more realism to your mounts. The more you learn, the more you earn, and *Taxidermy Review* is another good journal that should be on your monthly reading list.

Taxidermy Today, published by Terry Ehrlich, adds another dimension to taxidermy. Ehrlich is one of the noted professionals in the field of taxidermy, having won state and regional competitions for his artistic ability and creative renderings. Ehrlich's magazine is full of practical, "how-to" information that is easily adaptable to many situations. Between the covers of *Taxidermy Today*, the searching taxidermist will find additional ideas for making more money.

Tim Kelly, the editor of *American Taxidermist*, is also a professional taxidermist. Because of his involvement in providing a magazine for the trade and his participation in the NTA, Kelly frequents taxidermy studios around the country where he gleans novel but proven methods to disseminate to other taxidermists. Kelly, like most of the other editors, often asks various taxidermists to write articles—complete with illustrations—on their favorite mounting techniques or new and different ideas for making more money in the trade.

Professional taxidermists share ideas in the monthly trade magazines that will provide you a continuing source of new and unusual ideas to make more money in taxidermy. The constant flow of suggestions will spark your imagination and lead you down the trail to additional income that others in the profession may have discovered already. Or, you may be inspired with a fresh concept no one else has unearthed. If you want to continue to build a business and make more money, reading and studying the professional journals and attending the NTA conventions are musts.

(29) AD AGENCIES CAN TOTAL DOLLARS FOR YOU. If you live close to a large city or have a telephone directory from a nearby large city, look in the Yellow Pages under "Advertising Agencies." Simply drop each agency a letter explaining that you are a taxidermist with skins and mounted animals available for rent if they are interested in using them to promote any product or service. Also include the information that you are an outdoor consultant and will be happy to assist them in any advertising campaigns or product promotions dealing with the outdoors. Be sure to send the same letter to all the agencies. You may not see immediate results, but your letter will be kept on file. If any of your mounted specimens or your expertise can be used, you may be able to make some good money. It only takes the cost of a postage stamp to find out.

(30) BUYING BIG. All taxidermy supply houses, panel dealers, and form makers give quantity discounts for large orders. So you naturally think that buying your supplies in large amounts is better because you save money on the discounts and shipping. However, this assumption may not always be true. When you buy large quantities of supplies and have your money tied up in materials for an extended period of time, often you do not have use of your capital when you need it. Unless your business is extremely large with plenty of money available to tie up in supplies, forget about the quantity discounts. Let your money work for you while you keep a good inventory of what you need for the upcoming month on hand. When ordering supplies you can save dollars by sending a certified check, money order, or personal check so no COD charges must be paid.

(31) SERVICE IS STILL THE KEY TO ADDITIONAL DOLLARS AFTER THE SPECIMEN IS COMPLETED. As expensive as freight charges are for you, they are equally expensive for your customers. Just

consider the large boxes that most completed specimens have to be shipped in and the fact that the boxes must be transported by bus or truck lines.

There is a more economical way to ship for your customers while making extra dollars for yourself if you have several specimens going to one location. You can charge an additional fee for delivery service rather than using common carriers and explain to your customer that this ensures a safer arrival of his finished trophy for a smaller fee. If you have four or five mounts to go to the same city, you can carry them all at one time or get a friend to, and collect the money yourself that they would have paid out in freight charges. This money-making idea is especially helpful if you own an economy station wagon or truck.

Several years ago one of my customers who lived 200 miles away shipped me six deer heads for mounting. Upon completing the heads, we discovered that the cost to ship them back to him would be in excess of $225.00. To save him money and make a profit for myself, I loaded the six specimens in my small station wagon, which gets 36 miles to the gallon, and delivered them in person. The customer was glad to pay the $150.00 I charged to deliver the heads as opposed to the $225.00 he would have had to pay if the specimens had been shipped. I enjoyed the trip and spent less than $30.00 on gas. Service is an all-important factor in the taxidermy trade. Most customers would rather pay your expenses for delivering the specimens to them than the prices freight lines charge.

(32) DOCTORS ARE NOT THE ONLY ONES ON CALL. I have known taxidermists who made it almost impossible for customers to do business with them. One taxidermist I knew regulated his business by his freezer space. He had two freezers. When they were full of work he abruptly told his customers, "My freezers are full. If you can wait two or three months until I get some of the work out of them and bring your specimen to me then, I will mount it. If you can't wait and take care of the specimen yourself, take your work to somebody else," and in many cases that is exactly what the customer did. I have known other taxidermists who only came to their shops when they could not go hunting or fishing. They let their recreational activities dictate their business hours, and therefore they lost business. Taxidermy is a service-oriented profession. We have to be available when customers have work for us to do. For this reason the more available you are to customers in need, the more work you will receive.

(33) DOLLARS IN YOUR FREEZER. A freezer is one of the most essential items in a taxidermist's shop and can be one of the biggest money-makers you employ. Many sportsmen have a problem with what

Want to add a convenience that could mean more profit? Place an old freezer on your front porch so sports can leave their specimens when you're closed.

to do with a trophy after they have taken it. Most taxidermists hate to get out of bed at 11:00 at night to meet a customer at their studio. However, we taxidermists do need the money this customer brings. The solution may be a freezer on the front porch of your shop which enables you to receive specimens 24 hours a day.

Be sure to supply tags and wires so the sportsman can leave

information concerning the way he wants the animal mounted as well as his name, address, and telephone number. Keep current price lists available on the porch so there will be no question about fees.

Another way a freezer can benefit the taxidermist is to leave it at a sporting goods store, hunting club, preserve, or fishing camp where sportsmen can store specimens until you can come around to pick them up. I do not agree with giving agent kickbacks. However, if a service center or sporting goods shop wants to add on a handling and storage charge to my original fee, I have no problem with it. You may be surprised at how many people prefer to leave the handling of their deer to someone else. They would rather pay a set fee and let the other person take care of the details, such as storing the head and shipping it. By making the freezer available to your customers 24 hours a day, seven days a week, you increase the availability of your service.

One caution in using a freezer: Do not allow it to fill up with specimens on which you are not going to work.

Some folks will say, "Just leave my hide in your freezer when you get through cutting the cape off to mount. I plan to tan the hide myself, and I will come back in a few days to pick it up." Most taxidermists do not mind providing this small service for people who help feed our families. But you will have a problem when the customer does not come back in a few days for his hide, and you have eight or 10 other customers doing the same thing.

Or someone may say, "I want to leave my meat in your freezer for a day or two until I can find space in my refrigerator for it." Providing this service is also fine until the meat gets stacked on top of the hides we are waiting for people to pick up. Then if two more customers come in with large deer heads they cannot decide about mounting, the deer heads go on top of the meat that is sitting on top of the scalps. Before long you do not have any room in the freezer for the customers who have work to be done. To solve these problems we tell all our clients that we will be happy to hold their items in our freezer for one week. But at the end of that week they must pick up their property or we will dispose of it as we have limited freezer space to store items people do not plan to have mounted.

(34) LET THEM WORK WHILE YOU SLEEP. A taxidermist who is unavailable to his customers will soon be out of work. Being able to find out the prices you charge to mount specimens, knowing what to do with the specimen once they have taken it, and knowing when to pick up the finished work is critical information your customers must have to do business with you. At one time I solved the problem by having my business open seven days a week. I worked six days and had an employee available on Sundays. However, this is very costly. Then, by using an

answering system, I was able to delete two days from my work week at the office. In two days my answering service paid for itself for the entire deer season by answering customers' questions and taking messages for me.

Several types of answering services are available on the market today. I prefer the kind where an individual answers the telephone for you, has all the prices and instructions that you or your secretary would normally have for your customer, and has the ability to patch a caller through to wherever you are in case of emergency or some situation for which you have not left instructions. This type of service can be as personal as you desire, plus it allows your business to function 24 hours a day. Make sure you are dealing with a reputable answering service and that you have personal talks with the manager of the company and the head operator about the importance of getting the information across to the customer.

I have found that answering machines lack the ability to make decisions and handle your customers in an individual way. A few dollars paid out on a quality human answering service is money well spent and a key to making more money because you are offering better service to your customer.

(35) DON'T FORGET YOUR PRESENT CUSTOMERS WHILE TRYING TO GET NEW ONES. A fellow owned a fish market up the street from my taxidermy business. Each day I watched a steady flow of customers stream in and out of his store. Hard times, high prices, and poor business conditions never seemed to affect the fish market man's business adversely. One day, out of curiosity, I asked him his philosophy of business. He told me to watch. As I observed, every customer got a special price for that day. Each patron always went home with more than he thought he could purchase. The fish salesman said:

> If you'll remember this, boy, you will always be a success in any business venture you go into: Always take care of the customers you have first. These are the people who will continue to bring you business over the years. They are a captured market. You already have them, they already bring you business, and they encourage their friends to be a part of your business. Make sure you serve them first and best before you attempt to get new business. Always be certain you do a little something extra for them for which they did not pay. Attempt to make them a part of your business rather than just your business. Make sure when they come into your store that they come not only to bring work and money, but to meet a friend they have known over the years.

The advice was good, the philosophy was sound, and by implementing what the fish market proprietor said, my business has grown. One of the best methods I have found to "Keep the ones I have" is to stay in touch with them and let them know that I still want their business. We mail out letters twice a year to our taxidermy customers. We keep the name, address, and telephone number of each customer. Four to six weeks before deer season opens, I write a letter to all my customers. This letter usually contains the deer-hunting forecast I have obtained by calling the wildlife biologist in the state department of conservation. The letter tells my customers the best areas of my state to look for trophy deer, besides hunting tactics that have paid off for some of my customers in preceding years. Then, just to make sure that the letter is read and possibly used, I try to include two or three recipes for cooking wild meat that the customers may not have seen or tried before.

In closing the letter, I tell my customers how very much I have appreciated their business in the past, that I am looking forward to working for them in the upcoming season, and that they should feel free to call on me if I can be of any assistance. The helpful hints and recipes let my customers know that I am concerned about them and hope to get their taxidermy work. I also enclose two or three of my business cards that give current prices, my address, and shipping instructions. I have found that by mailing this letter to previous customers prior to the season, I increase my repeat business substantially. Many of my patrons mention the information I sent them or the suggestions I made when they come in with their specimens.

During the fishing season I follow the same procedure in dealing with the customers who have brought in fish to be mounted during the past two to three years. This technique reassures the customer that I am interested in him, that I do want his business, and that I am willing to serve him. Often we make the assumption that once a sportsman has brought us work he will continue to do so. But I think this is incorrect. I believe hunters and fishermen do business with people they know, whose work they respect, and who have become friends as well as servants. The philosophy of the fish market salesman, who advised taking care of the ones you already have before going in search of new business, is true. By incorporating this philosophy into your taxidermy business you will see added dollars in your cash register at the end of each season.

(36) REPAIR WORK—SHOULD YOU DO IT? Repair work has been a thorn in the sides of most taxidermists all of their business lives. Usually we do not mind repairing our own work if there is a problem with it. But fixing somebody else's work is like giving the neighbor's child a bath. You will do it because the child needs it, but you would rather not. Because of this quirk in taxidermists, many professionals turn down volumes of work simply because there is some kind of stigma about repairing someone else's specimen. However, remember that these people have a problem

that the man who mounted their specimen either could not or would not solve. They have come to you for help. If, in the process of repairing their specimens, you make a friend and do as good a job as can be done, this potential customer will remember you the next time he has a specimen to be mounted.

Often a deer head may fall off the wall or a set of antlers be broken while moving them. In either case, the taxidermist willing do repair work can find additional dollars by meeting this need and can pick up new customers as well.

Always make sure to charge enough to cover the cost of your time and materials used in making the repairs. But do not overcharge the customer like some taxidermists do in an attempt to penalize the customer for taking his work to someone else to begin with and in hopes of discouraging other repair business. By following this line of thinking, many potentially good customers will steer business away from this taxidermist with remarks like, "I would have taken my specimen to ole Billy Bob to be mounted, but he charged me so much for a little repair job on a duck that I know he would be higher than anybody else if I took him a deer head or fish to mount."

This was a captured customer lost by a taxidermist who did not put serving his customer ahead of his own likes and dislikes.

(37) ADVERTISING CAN MAKE OR BREAK YOU. Most businessmen know the value of advertising. Generating business is difficult if no one knows you are in business. But what type of advertising works best for a taxidermist? What is the least expensive form of advertising, and how much do you actually need to spend to promote your business? These are questions many taxidermists fail to evaluate.

A prime example of not evaluating the best kinds of advertising is one of my friends who takes in a tremendous volume of specimens each year. He advertises on a local radio station and in sporting magazines. He discounts his work to some hunting clubs who are responsible for a large volume of his business. He gives away a considerable number of mounts each year in an attempt to bring in more business. At the end of the season when he subtracts his advertising budget and his overhead expenses from the amount of revenue he has received the books will not balance.

Taxidermists must evaluate advertising expenses along these lines:

1. If a duck costs $10.00 to mount, and you got the specimen for free and then gave it away for advertising consideration, then most of us would assume you had a $10.00 expense involved in putting that duck on display. However, this is a false concept. If you charge $50.00 or $60.00 to mount a duck for a customer and it takes you the same amount of time to mount that advertising duck, then instead of having spent $10.00 for advertising, you in fact have spent $40.00 or $50.00. With the same amount of time and materials you expended creating display work, you could have earned the retail price of a specimen. So when calculating advertising costs to determine your expenses, list the expense at the retail value of the specimen rather than at material cost only.

2. When friends, relatives, and business acquaintances want you to

discount your work for them, ask yourself this question: Would that same customer expect me to discount my merchandise if I were working in a retail store rather than a taxidermy shop? In most cases, the answer is no. After you have determined what a fair and equitable price is to ask for your work, you should charge that price. When you receive less than your normal charges for your skills, you deliberately are taking money out of your pocket and your family's budget and giving it away to your customers. One rule of thumb to always consider when giving away free mounts or discounting work is that if your customers can be bought by cheap work or work at no charge, someone else can buy them for the same price. The best rule of thumb is to set one price for all and charge everyone the same rate.

One of the best advertising tools I have ever heard of involves scrap rawhide and turkey feathers and the cost is negligible. Larry Blomquist explained this tactic to me:

> We usually have a lot of tanned deerskin scraps around the shop. These will be left over when we cover elk and moose antlers and the 101 other things for which we use deerskin. We take these scraps of leather, cut them into one-inch wide strips, and glue them together so they make a circle. Then we staple or glue a turkey feather on the back. On the front of the leather with a felt pen we write *Blomquist Taxidermy*. All the kids who come in with their daddies when they bring their specimens receive one of these genuine Indian headbands. The kids really enjoy them. Our customers seem to appreciate the little extra attention their children receive when they bring their specimens to us.
>
> And although this form of advertising really doesn't cost anything it sure does build a lot of goodwill. I believe the headbands create repeat business, because we have customers who years later write or call and ask if we have an extra Indian headband for one of their younger children who wasn't big enough to get one of his own the last time Daddy killed a deer.

Some may say that their best form of advertising is their work. I wholeheartedly agree with this philosophy, assuming the taxidermist does quality work. However, if a potential customer sees and admires your craft but fails to know or find out who mounted the trophy he is viewing, then that specimen will generate no business. I always attach advertising decals, nameplates or a rubber stamp impression on the back of the panel or mounting board of every specimen that leaves my business. If your customer does not want a nameplate, you can place a small decal on the bottom of the panel with the words "Mounted by," followed by your name, address, and telephone number. If there is no room for a decal or nameplate at the base of the panel, attach it to the back of the plaque.

Another effective and inexpensive technique of advertising is the use of posters. A good poster that contains sharp black-and-white photographs of your work allows you to show off your skills, gives the necessary information to direct clients to your business, and provides shipping information to your customers who live too far to bring the specimens to you. Posters in tackle shops, roadside grocery stores, hunting clubs, and meat markets are an effective way to advertise your business and let people know where to find you.

Many taxidermists place advertising specimens in various locations. But some fish and animals are so costly to mount that the possibility of receiving enough return to justify the display does not warrant their use. For example, a sailfish represents a large investment of a taxidermist's time and money. The same message may be communicated and a demonstration of the artist's work made visible by mounting a dolphin.

Deer heads are impressive, but they also require a lot of time and represent a larger expense for the taxidermist than a squirrel or duck. So the taxidermist who mounts deer heads for display must increase his volume of business far more to justify this expense than does the taxidermist who mounts a duck for display. Again, remember when figuring your advertising budget that your expense in using some of your mounted work should be based on the retail cost of that specimen, not in the material cost.

Also, an unkempt display can actually be negative advertising. A taxidermist must check the specimens in his displays on a regular basis to replace damaged or discolored items with clean mounts.

As for finding a place to display work, there are takers on every corner. I have known taxidermists who allowed merchants to dictate how much of their work they should display. A prime example is a leading sporting goods store I visited a few seasons ago. I approached the manager of the sporting goods department and asked if he would mind if I left my cards and a poster in his store.

"Not at all, we'll be glad to refer customers to you," he said. "Leave us plenty of cards. We'll put your poster right up on the register. By the way, we need to get some of your work to display. Let's see, we'll need a couple of fox to go up over the guncase, a bobcat would look nice in our clothing department, how about a couple of ducks we could hang behind the register and three nice deer heads to hang from each one of the columns in the sporting goods department?"

"Sure," I told the man. "I'll be glad to do it. Then I want you to give me one of those brand new Weatherby 300 Magnum rifles, a Remington Model 1100 shotgun with two barrels, and throw in three cases of No. 6 shot High Brass shells to go with it. Let's see now, I'll need a cabin tent and an Old Town Tripper canoe."

"You mean you want to buy all that equipment?" the startled man asked.

"Oh, no, I want you to give it to me," I told him.

A look of disbelief was on the man's face as he said, "We can't give you that merchandise."

"Why not?" I asked. "You wanted me to give you the equivalent of those goods in free displays of my work. I just thought this would be an even trade."

"Yes, but we're going to tell people to bring business to you at the taxidermy shop," the man replied.

"Well, if you'll give me all the stuff I want, I'll tell each sportsman who comes through my shop to buy their hunting and fishing supplies from you," I said seriously.

The manager was in total shock. He had assumed that like other taxidermists he had "worked" with in the past, I would give him any of the specimens he wanted for display for the honor of having him refer business to me. I have fallen into this trap before and so have a lot of other taxidermist friends of mine. In the final evaluation, I always have found that I rarely have recovered the cost of the specimens I put on display, much less received any benefit when I have given away large volume of display work.

That same sporting goods manager probably will offer a similar deal to any other taxidermist who comes into his store whether my work is up or not. This kind of unscrupulous businessman will take advantage of you and can teach you how to make less money in taxidermy.

Along these same lines may be the big-time professional hunter or fisherman who decides to bless you by referring business to you. All that he wants in return is for you to mount a few fish and/or a few animals for free. In some cases, these sportsmen are true to their word and will not take advantage of you by expecting you to mount more than a reasonable number of specimens for free or at a cut rate. However, my experience has been that often this type of outdoorsman will permit you to do any abundance of work for him, send you a small amount of business in return, and, as soon as he has a sufficient number of trophies, he will find another taxidermist to court.

Remember what was said earlier. Any business that can be bought with a free mount can be bought by somebody else for two free mounts. I never have found that giving away work to individuals in an attempt to lure additional business brought in more dollars than it cost. The most effective form of advertising in taxidermy—as it is in so many other professions—is a well-satisfied customer who believes in you and your talent.

(38) PATCH YOUR WAY TO SUCCESS. The latest fad with many sportsmen is patches—patches to denote big deer, trophy bass, tournaments they have fished in, or accomplishments they have achieved. I have seen outdoorsmen spend hundreds of dollars to earn a patch to wear on their jackets or hats so all their friends will know they have either done something, won something, or been somewhere. All the major tackle and outdoor companies give away and sell product patches that sportsmen wear on their hunting and fishing attire. The taxidermist who recognizes the advertising benefits of the outdoor patch can put his name inexpensively in front of a large number of sportsmen at a very low price.

I started a patch program for my taxidermy business a few years ago when I contacted Ted Salters of EBSCO Industries, Outdoors Division, 1301 First Ave. N, Birmingham, AL 35203. Ted designed a patch for me with a deer head in the center, my name across the bottom, and "Big Buck Award" in large letters across the top. I decided to give this patch to any customer who brought in a deer to be mounted that was 10 points or better. The John Phillips' Big Buck Award patch has succeeded in putting my name before sportsmen all over the state and has become a walking advertisement for my business. The same type of program will work equally as well on fish or other trophies.

In lieu of a patch program, some taxidermists present their customers with hats to be worn in the field that carry the taxidermist's name, address, and telephone number. I believe that any type of walking advertisement you can attach to your customer at a nominal cost—whether it is a patch, pin, button, badge, hat, jacket, or shirt—will carry your message to the people who are the most interested in your business. However, a patch that carries a degree of honor with it, such as the Big Buck Award, is far more valuable to the sportsman and will be more readily displayed than a patch that just bears your company's name.

(39) TAKE THE BUS AND LEAVE THE DRIVING TO US. After a taxidermy business has been built to a certain point, it usually will stay at that level unless the taxidermist is smart enough to solicit business outside his own region. The biggest problem with receiving specimens is choosing the right means of transportation so the trophy will not be spoiled by the time it arrives at the taxidermist. Below is a list of findings after years of research on this subject:

1. Parcel Post and United Parcel Service (UPS). These are good methods for shipping tanned skins and small mounted trophies, but we have found them to be too slow for fresh specimens.

2. Railroad. This is also too slow a means for transporting fresh specimens to the taxidermist, but can be utilized for critters already mounted.

3. Air Freight. This is okay, but still not the best. Many times a specimen will sit in an airport for a day or two before it is shipped. We also have found that sometimes the airport will wait a day or so before calling to notify us that we have a box waiting.

4. Bus Lines. This is the best, safest, and quickest way to receive specimens. Our instructions to our customers read as follows and are printed on our business cards and posters:

   a. Freeze your trophy solid.
   b. Wrap it in two inches of newspaper.
   c. Put it in a cardboard box.
   d. Put your name, address, and telephone number on the outside of the box.
   e. Mark in permanent ink with a felt-tipped pen, "Call On Arrival—John Phillips, Taxidermist, 207 51st St., Fairfield, AL 35064, Ph: 205-786-4022, 786-3630."
   f. Attach an envelope to the outside of the box with all the mounting instructions; shipping instructions; your name, address, and telephone number, and nameplate information.

In our studio in Alabama we have received specimens from New York, California, and Canada that still have to be unthawed when they arrive at our shop after being shipped by bus. The day we take in someone's shipment, we immediately forward the following letter to them after checking the animal over carefully. We have the letters "quick printed" and ready for our use. All we have to do is fill in the blanks.

Date:

Dear

Just thought I'd drop you a note and let you know that we have received your shipment. We certainly do appreciate your business. We will be shipping your _____ as soon as it is completed. Our service time for _____ runs _____ to _____ months, with the items received at the first of the season being completed first. Please feel free to contact us if we can be of any help to you. Thank you again for your valued business.

Sincerely yours,

John E. Phillips
Taxidermist
Received _____ on _____

Along with the letter, we send a price list and some business cards for the out-of-towner to pass on to his friends. The letter provides another chance for us to contact the customer, assures him that everything is going to be fine with his mount, and presents a more professional appearance for our business.

For returning trophies to our customers we use UPS, bus lines, or freight lines according to the size of the shipment and best price available. Prior to returning the specimen, we drop the customer a letter telling him that his trophy has been completed, stating the balance he owes, and asking that he send a check or money order for the money due. This procedure guards against several problems:

1. It prevents our customer from having to pay additional COD fees.
2. It assures us that we will get paid for our work.
3. It avoids the situation where a specimen is shipped but the customer fails to pick it up, which has occurred in the past. In those cases, we had to absorb the expense of mounting the specimen, which we did not get paid for, as well as the cost of shipping the mount two ways— once to the customer and also when the specimen was returned to us.

By utilizing the above procedure of writing and notifying before you ship, you also ensure that the customer will have the money available when the specimen is ready.

(40) HELP. One of the biggest drains on any taxidermy business is help. Employees can often represent a larger expenditure than most of us are willing to admit. Like many other professionals I have been guilty of creating work to keep a job available for an employee. I also have allowed employees to do jobs I could have and would have done if they had not been there. If you are to make more money in taxidermy, you must be able to regulate your help so that your employees represent a profit center rather than an outgoing expense.

The general rule of thumb I have found works best when considering hiring additional help is when I am doing all I can by working six days a week, 10 hours a day, and still cannot catch up. At that point I consider hiring additional help. However, do not overlook the fact that some taxidermists are at their businesses 10 hours a day, six days a week, but are not working. I know many taxidermists who could mount two to three deer heads a day, yet they choose to only mount one. Therefore, even though they are putting in long hours, they actually are working very little. If you are putting in the number of hours that seem to justify additional employees, look at your schedule again and see if by hustling a

Good help may be hard to find, but you'd be surprised how many people are looking to earn a few extra dollars these days. Housewives, retired persons, and young people interested in after-school work are good prospects. Here Archie Phillips shows Tammy Manley the art of bass skinning.

little more you can produce more work in the same number of hours that you are spending in your shop. Once you determine you are working as fast as you possibly can, as long as you can, and are still unable to get your work out as quickly as you want to, then the only reasonable conclusion you can make is to hire an extra employee.

After the decision is made to add personnel, a taxidermist must realize that his own productivity will be drastically reduced during the first few weeks or months as his new worker learns. Training and mistakes will eat away at your time while you are instructing the new employee in his duties. You should have a clear-cut picture of what the employee can do to make you more efficient and to enable you to really increase the volume of work you are able to put out during a given period of time.

But what kind of employee should you look for and where can you find the right one? I believe the most profitable and best-run taxidermy businesses in America are family owned. Family loyalty, family pride, and family concern tend to bring out the characteristics in a business and in work that pay the highest dividends, not only monetarily but in the quality of workmanship. An immediate family member often will work for less and produce more than someone outside the family. Sons and daughters can learn from their fathers and mothers, are much quicker to accept criticism, and tend to be more concerned about the business than employees not related to the family. I believe that the family-operated taxidermy business is the most effective and profitable way to practice this art.

Local teenagers represent another excellent source of help. A mature teenager may prove to be a good employee. Young people have a difficult time finding work. Even though these youngsters may be highly motivated, dexterous, and willing to work, many employers will not tap this labor pool. It has been my experience that a young person who grows in a business and learns your procedures and skills may one day become a valuable employee in your taxidermy shop.

Since taxidermy is an artistic form requiring sewing, modeling, painting, and decorating skills, I have found that women also make good employees. Many women are better at working with their hands and pay closer attention to detail than other employees. If they have families, they may prefer part-time work during the hours their children are in school. So the taxidermist can employ these workers as parttime help during the morning hours when the teenagers are in school. Both groups of employees can skin, flesh, mount, and do the other tasks with equal skill.

I once had a woman come to the shop and exclaim "Ooh," and "Aah" when I showed her how deer and other animals are skinned.

"How do you stand to touch those 'things'?" she questioned.

I asked her what she did for a living.

"Oh, I'm a nurse," she explained.

With that I laughed so hard she wanted to know what was so funny.

"Well, in my opinion, human beings are about the nastiest things a person can work with and especially sick ones," I said. "Sick humans

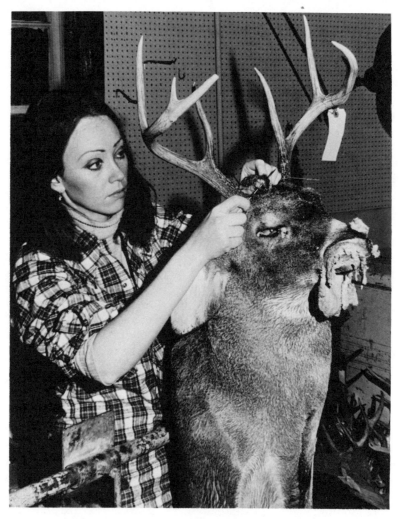

A woman good with needle and thread might be eager to use her talents to earn extra dollars working for you.

smell bad, throw up, and have bedpans to be emptied. Matter of fact, I haven't handled an animal that ever smelled half as bad as a human that was sick."

After a closer investigation into our work, she had to agree that her customers were a lot more undesirable than our specimens. Usually after a woman employee gets over the idea that skinning or mounting an animal, bird, or fish is distasteful she becomes the best of help. Women may develop into the better taxidermists than men.

(41) HANDLING COMPLAINTS. A dissatisfied customer will not continue to bring his business to you, and he also may prevent anyone within earshot from bringing his work to you. Therefore, if you are to make more money in taxidermy you must be able to handle complaints and satisfy customers.

At my office we will do whatever is required to solve a customer's problem whether the problem stems from an error on our part or his part. A prime example involved an old man and a boy who came into our shop one day. The elderly hunter had a tremendous 10-point buck that had been shot twice in the neck with birdshot besides being split from his brisket up the front of his neck to the tip of his chin and cut from ear to ear.

"Nobody will mount this deer," the old man told me. "Several other taxidermists have told me that you are the only one who would possibly mount the head."

I knew when I saw the specimen that more work would be required than I could possibly get paid for the mount. However, we mounted the head, made a friend, and subsequently received more business not only from that man but from all his friends. In that case, solving the problem was easy because the customer had created the problem.

One solution that is not so easy to solve is when the taxidermist has made the problem. A customer came in to pick up his deer head and found that it was turned the wrong way.

"I specifically asked that my deer look to the right. You have him mounted looking to the left," the customer explained.

We checked the mounting instructions tag and found that the man was correct. I had made an honest mistake. The trophy was not mounted the way the customer had requested, and I was at fault. This was a very bad situation to find myself in, but one that will surely happen to you if you stay in taxidermy—no matter how careful you are. No amount of explanation seemed to satisfy the irate sportsman. Apologies were not accepted and the situation progressed from bad to worse. Finally I told the man that I would do whatever was required to not only satisfy him but to maintain him as a customer and to let him know that I wanted to continue to serve him.

"Well, I think it would be fair if you mount my next deer head for less than the full price," the man suggested.

I agreed to do that and asked how much less he thought would be fair.

After thinking awhile he said, "If you will take $25.00 off my next mount, I will feel that you have dealt fairly with me."

I gladly would have given the man the mount for free since I was in error. However, that was not what he required to be satisfied. But to go one step further and assure him of my sincerity, I said, "Would you feel

73

that I have been more than fair if I give you $50.00 off your next mount? I want you to have the best end of this bargain since I made the mistake."

The man could not believe the offer. But he graciously accepted. I saved his business, and he continued to bring friends with their specimens for me to mount.

Often a taxidermist will have problems he knows nothing about, until everybody in town has heard them. Three or four years after a specimen has been mounted, a problem may develop with it. A mounted deer head may have been placed over a fireplace, and the heat generated from the flames may have caused the head to become discolored or the hide to crack. A bird hung in a high ceiling can become discolored from dirt or dust or the ear of a fox may be broken, making it unsuitable for display. No matter what the cause of a customer's dissatisfaction, the taxidermist's business will be adversely affected if this attitude persists. For this reason, we offer a lifetime guarantee on all our work. At any time that a customer has a problem with work we have performed, we will do whatever is required to rectify that problem to satisfy the customer. Customer satisfaction is the key ingredient in generating additional revenue in the taxidermy business.

(42) THE COMPETITION CAN MAKE YOU MONEY. In some cases your competitors can be your best source of revenue if you develop a friendly relationship with them and refrain from trying to discredit them in the eyes of other people. A competitor may have a call on a job that he does not want to perform. So, knowing you will mount anything, he may send the specimen to you if the two of you have an esprit de corps.

And if you stay in taxidermy long enough, you will see many competitors come and go over the years. Each one will build up centers of influence and have regular customers. When these taxidermists conclude their careers, their customers will continue to call and want to bring them work. Once these customers learn that their friend is no longer a taxidermist, they will ask him to recommend someone else to handle their specimens. If you have established a good relationship with your competitors, you may be the one that the work is referred to instead of someone else. I have had taxidermists turn over all their unmounted specimens and customers to me once they made the decision to no longer participate in taxidermy. Keep this in mind. Your competitors may be willing to put dollars in your pocket if you do not alienate them by trying to discredit their work.

(43) DISPLAY TAXIDERMY. As discussed earlier in this book, there are some pitfalls with display taxidermy including failing to realize the expense you incur with display taxidermy and letting the store owner dictate to you what or how many specimens to display.

However, I have watched the largest freshwater fish taxidermy studio in the world grow from display taxidermy. Every spring for almost 20 years, my brother, Archie, has loaded hundreds of mounted bass in his pickup truck and traveled the United States. The method he uses for display advertising is quite simple. Archie goes into an area and inquires as to the best sporting goods dealer, marina operator, and fishing guide in the locale. Some places have as many as 12 to 15 qualified prospects, and some have only one. But whoever the center of influence is, Archie goes to see the man, introduces himself and his business, and tries to establish a rapport.

Perhaps the man will say, "We already have a local taxidermist, John Doe, who does most of our work."

To this Archie will reply, "That's fine. We would just like to give you one of our sample fish for display. Would you mind letting your customers make the decision as to who they want to mount their fish and ship them to us if they choose?"

Remember, never cut down or try to belittle your competition. This serves only to make you look small. Display your work and let the customer make the decision. As you can see, this is a very time-consuming and expensive means of advertising, but it does have proven results.

Joseph Bruchac of Greenfield Center, New York, publisher of *Modern Taxidermy,* has an excellent idea along the lines of display taxidermy:

> Many sporting good dealers and outdoor shops want mounted work for display. Then when you get it back from them the display is usually broken or damaged in some way. Because they are allowed to have your work for nothing, to them it has no value and often is abused. I have found that a good way to make more money in taxidermy is to rent out your specimens. Charge a weekly or monthly fee for your work, plus tell your customers that they are responsible for all damages and will be charged for any repairs that have to be made. This arrangement gives your work value and ensures that you will be compensated for any damage done to your specimens.

According to Bruchac, this is a lucrative business for a taxidermist who has access to large cities where sporting good stores, marinas, and restaurants abound.

(44) MAKE MONEY WITH ENGRAVED NAMEPLATES. Bowling trophies, baseball trophies, and even knitting trophies all have engraved nameplates. A trophy in itself signifies only that some noteworthy accomplishment has been made. The nameplate tells what the accomplishment was, who accomplished the feat, and when and where the activity took place.

Many taxidermists overlook the making of nameplates as a source of additional income for the taxidermy business. Some taxidermists make from $500.00 to $3000.00 extra each year by using nameplates under their trophies. Many suppliers furnish nameplates to the taxidermy trade (see "Taxidermy Supply Sources" in the Appendix). You can acquire nameplates for as little as $2.50 each or as much as $8.00 to $9.00 each. Most customers will want the inscription to read "Killed by (or caught by)," followed by their name and the date and place that the trophy was taken. By adding the cost of the nameplate plus the cost of postage and a 50 percent charge for handling the order and attaching the plate to the plaque, you can bring in extra dollars to your taxidermy business.

Nameplates may even be sold to customers whom you never see, although you mount their specimens. When you return a mounted trophy by freight or bus lines to a customer in a faraway city, always include a few of your cards and your price list. If the customer has not asked for a nameplate, attach a card which reads:

> If you would like a trophy nameplate to be displayed under your mount, please fill out the following form and send it back to us with an $8.00 check or money order. Our mailing address is on the other side of this card. The plate should read:
>
> Caught By
> _____ (Name)
> _____ (Date)
> _____ (Place)

(45) FORTUNE IN FISH BLANKS. The answer to the question, "What can I do when I don't have any specimens to mount?" can be answered easily with fish blanks.

"What can I offer my customers when they bring in specimens that are ruined or spoiled?" The answer is fish blanks.

"How can I sell display fish to a seafood restaurant chain when I am 1000 miles from the coast and the chances of my acquiring a specimen to mount are impossible?" The answer is fish blanks.

Fish blanks are fiberglass reproductions of real fish. A good blank has great details and in many cases is almost impossible to distinguish from a skin-mounted fish. Because fiberglass reproductions may seem foreign or new to many taxidermists or because the taxidermist has no skill or knowledge in working with the fiberglass reproductions, many dollars are often lost. Another excellent reason for learning how to work with fiberglass reproductions is to solve the age-old problem of oil leaking out of saltwater specimens. Most taxidermists who mount saltwater species rely heavily on fiberglass reproductions. Many taxidermists who mount thin-skinned trout prefer to use fiberglass reproductions as well. You should investigate the feasibility of using fish blanks in your work.

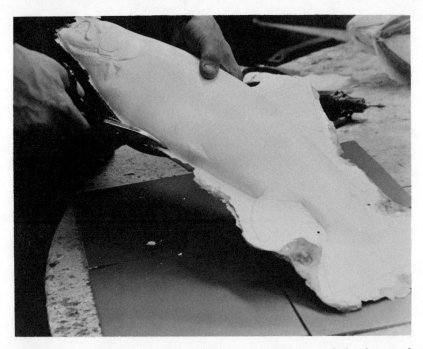

Fish blanks are fiberglass reproductions of real fish, and they're used extensively these days, especially with saltwater species. You should learn to work with them to expand your business.

There are several suppliers of fiberglass fish blanks. The accompanying pictures show you just how easy fish blanks are to use.

As I mentioned earlier, once you have your fiberglass reproduction completed and painted, an excellent place to sell it is at seafood restaurants. Most restaurants that specialize in seafood have found that mounted fish add to the decor of their establishment. There may also be sporting goods shops and outdoor stores that would appreciate the opportunity to purchase a large fiberglass reproduction. The 27-inch California bass that weighed 21 pounds is available in a fiberglass reproduction. Or you may enjoy mounting a 411-pound blue marlin that has been perfectly molded in fiberglass. How many eyes would pop if they saw the fiberglass reproduction of the 1947 World's Record Bream taken from Lake Ketona in Alabama that weighed four pounds, 10 ounces? Another big panfish available in fiberglass is a 17-inch shell-cracker (red-eared sunfish) from North Carolina that weighed approximately 5.5 pounds. A four-pound, six-ounce crappie also has been made in fiberglass. Trout fishermen will really begin to talk if they see a fiberglass reproduction of a 30-inch rainbow. Everybody likes sharks, so

FOR
SALE
$75.⁰⁰

A finished fiberglass mount is attractive and will last for ages. It'll also ring up nicely on your cash register.

for the taxidermist who wants a monster to display, how about a 500-pound bull shark, a 300-pound blacktip, a 400-pound hammerhead, or a 224-pound mako? There are fiberglass reproductions of almost all the major species including both fresh- and saltwater fish. The taxidermist who does not capitalize on this market is making a big mistake.

(46) DON'T DO IT FOR NOTHING. When you take a specimen in on which to perform your art, you have a degree of time and money tied up in that critter. If the customer does not come back to pick it up, then you eventually may sell it to cover your expenses. In the meantime, however, you still have your money involved in that particular job.

   In our studio we require a 50 percent deposit on all work before we start mounting. If the customer does not have a check or cash with him when he comes in, we allow two weeks for the deposit. We follow these guidelines:

1.   If the deposit does not come in within the two-week period, we send a general reminder to the customer.
2.   If two more weeks pass and we still have not received our deposit, we

send another letter stating that we must have the money in order to begin work on the animal and that this is the second notice. We also state a date when the money must be received by us.

3. If we do not get our deposit by the date specified in our second letter, we write a third and final letter. We certify this letter at the post office and request a signed receipt so we will know who accepted the letter. This letter states that if the deposit is not brought in within 10 days of the date of the letter, the specimen will be disposed of in our usual manner.

4. If the deposit is never received, all the correspondence is filed. Then we do whatever we want to with the critter. But we have been fair. We have given the customer eight to 10 weeks to send in the deposit. Also, if there is a problem with his paying, we are glad to work with our customers. Sometimes we have customers who pay $5.00 a week until they get their deposit paid off. Then we start work on the animal.

The above system may seem like a lot of secretarial work, but we use the following form letters with blanks to be filled in at the appropriate places for this type of correspondence. We either have the letters quick-copied or printed complete with our letterhead, address, and telephone number.

1. Our general reminder letter for a deposit reads:
   Date:
   Dear _____ :
   We do appreciate your bringing your _____ to us this season on _____ . In order to begin our mounting process on your animal, we must receive a deposit in the amount of _____ . Our freezer space is limited, and we must therefore ask your immediate attention to this matter of your deposit. Thank you again for your valued business.
   Yours truly,
   John E. Phillips
   Taxidermist

2. After sending the above letter, if we still have not received a deposit or a call explaining about the delay in the deposit, we send another copy of the above letter noting the date of the first notice and that this is the second notice.

3. If the customer does not respond in any way to the two above letters, we then send the following letter, certified, to the customer, after photocopying and filing it with the receipts from the post office. This certified letter reads:

Date:

Dear _____ :

We do appreciate your bringing your _____ to us this season on _____ . You were notified on _____ and _____ that we must receive a deposit in the amount of _____ in order to begin mounting the animal. We have limited storage space and are unable to hold animals for customers. Please let us hear from you or receive some money from you by _____ . We will have to dispose of your _____ in our usual manner if you have not contacted us by _____ . Thanking you in advance for your time and consideration, I remain,

Yours truly,

John E. Phillips

Taxidermist

(47) HABITAT MOUNTS. The taxidermist who wants to receive more money for his work should be willing to give his customer more work for his money. There are several methods of enhancing one's work.

First, spend the time to find natural plaques on which to mount many of your specimens. For instance, ducks look better on unfinished driftwood in many cases than they do on panels. A squirrel may appear more natural on an old piece of driftwood than it does on a stained plaque. A fox walking along a log will appear more real than he will on a finished board. The taxidermist may have to spend a day in the woods picking up mounting plaques and should charge extra for the effort.

To carry this same thought one step further, dried weeds and flowers can be added to the base to create a scene that more naturally resembles the animal's native habitat than a backboard or panel does. A strand of artificial ivy can make a raccoon climbing up a log look more lifelike than that same coon will on a bare log. Dried weeds and flowers arranged properly behind or in front of the mount will give the specimen more depth and make it more artistic.

Since most taxidermists have not had a course in flower arranging, nor do they know the different dried flowers available for them to use with their habitat scenes, the best source of help is the local florist. The florist, like the taxidermist, is often a very creative person who works in a different medium to portray beauty. The florist will know the proper shrubs and flowers, the correct height of materials, and the best way for you to show off your art by combining it with his expertise.

There are two routes that a taxidermist may choose when working with the florist:

1. Pay the florist to teach you how to utilize the flowers, bushes, shrubs, shells, and rocks you need to create a lifelike arrangement for your

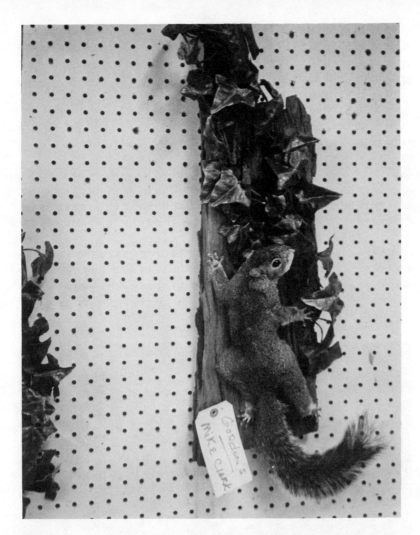

More and more sportsmen are going in for habitat, or natural setting displays such as this bushytail dressed up with a touch of artificial ivy. Some oak leaves and acorns could also be a nice arrangement.

habitat setting. You may want to buy your materials and supplies from your local florist, or you may choose to buy directly from a floral supply dealer, depending on the volume of work you anticipate doing with habitat arrangements.

2. You can mount your specimens, take them to the florist, let him do all the arrangement and habitat creation, and pass the additional expense along to your customer plus add in a profit for yourself.

Many fine restaurants and private clubs will welcome the opportunity to purchase a mounted pheasant in a habitat scene for a centerpiece at a large banquet table. Those wary of taxidermy items will accept mounted specimens in their homes more readily if the animal helps to create an illusion of the outdoors rather than appearing as something that is dead and stuffed. Using an artistic flair to create more of a semblance of life in your mounted specimens can reap large dividends and set you far above your competition.

(48) MUSEUM MOUNTS. Most taxidermists try to make their trophies appear as they would have in life. As craftsmen, we attempt to recreate life in dead trophies, but the artist/taxidermist also uses mounted specimens to capture a moment in time. This type of mounting is often referred to as museum taxidermy.

A museum mount is often one that not only includes the habitat that the specimen may be found in, but portrays him in action. An example would be a fox mounted with a quail in his mouth and other quail at his

Big projects can mean big bucks for the taxidermist. And it's really not difficult to make something like this quail shadow box for a hardwood desk.

feet, scurrying to escape or leaping to fly away. For a split second, the taxidermist has frozen the action of animals and birds in a struggle for survival. The fleeing quail, the dead bird in a fox's mouth—all surrounded by their natural habitat—truly reclassify taxidermy as art rather than craft. This type of mounting encompasses all the aspects of taxidermy and requires more time, skill, and specimens than would an ordinary fox mount. For this additional work, the taxidermist is obliged to charge higher prices. If an open-mouth fox mount normally costs $175.00, a quail costs $75.00, and the addition of the habitat is $35.00, it is easy to see how a taxidermist can receive more money by creating museum mounts than he does merely by mounting a fox. The customer who brings in a fox will spend $175.00. If the taxidermist can show that same customer a museum mount and assure him that he can purchase quail from a game ranch to be added to the mount, which will include also a habitat setting to make a museum mount, the taxidermist will have increased the amount of work he has by two quail and the habitat and added $185.00 to his pocket. Now instead of receiving $175.00 for mounting the fox, the taxidermist will get $360.00 for creating a museum

This wood duck coming in for a landing exemplifies the realistic approach to a mount.

83

mount and provide his customer with a higher quality, more natural and exciting mount than he originally requested.

As you can see, the possibilities are limitless. One of my favorite mounts is two squirrels coming down a tree. When I can find an old piece of wood that has a knothole in it, I enjoy doing this type of mount. The first squirrel is mounted below the knothole climbing down the tree in the usual position. Half of the second squirrel is mounted coming out of the knothole and attempting to come down the tree. Again the action of the two animals is frozen in one of their daily pursuits. We have increased the value of the mount and provided for our customer a more realistic portrayal of the animals he brought in for us to mount.

Ducks also lend themselves well to habitat-type mounting in museum style. By mounting one duck standing on a piece of driftwood, looking up as another duck attempts to land, the taxidermist can create a scene rather than merely mounting a specimen. Museum-type mounts seem to be the latest trend in taxidermy. They permit much more freedom and expression in the art than does standard mounting. The taxidermist who intends to incorporate this form into his work may have to learn some new skills and experiment with novel techniques in posing his specimens.

There is also a trend in fish taxidermy toward more natural mounts. Taxidermists are beginning to create underwater scenes utilizing driftwood and dried weeds to give the illusion of a subsurface display. In many cases a big bass will have his mouth open and his gills flared as he attacks a bluegill just below the surface. Above the fish and the driftwood, artificial lily pads and water lilies can be used to create the illusion of the surface so that a client has a three-dimensional scene of his trophy in the act of foraging for food. Other taxidermists mount trout under rocks or looking up through glass at a bug that may be glued to the surface. Stringer mounts have gained in popularity and add an artistic flair to fish mounting.

Some taxidermists have mounted a dead trout lying across a log with a fox mount to simulate the fox's having caught the fish. I believe that the future of the taxidermy profession and the way to make more money in taxidermy may very well be in this direction.

(49) WHOLESALE TAXIDERMY. Most taxidermists encounter two very basic problems in their businesses: (1) What do you do when you do not have any specimens to mount? and (2) What do you do when you have too many specimens to mount?

The answer to both questions is the same—wholesale taxidermy. The taxidermist who does not have enough to do should determine what most taxidermists in his area do not enjoy mounting. Taxidermists are like anyone else. The work they do not like to do, they tend to put off until

Museum mounts usually involve more than one specimen and should stop action as if the fish or game were frozen in time. This big-bellied bass coming up to inhale the spinnerbait beneath the lilypads is a fine example.

later. The specimens they enjoy mounting, they mount first and most often. Consequently, many taxidermists have a backlog of specimens that they do not want to mount. Yet they have had them for a long period of time and need to complete them and move them out of their shops. A taxidermist with a problem is just like a customer with a problem. He is willing to pay someone to eliminate that problem. So here is a niche that the taxidermist who does not have enough work to do can fill.

For instance, some taxidermists do not like to mount birds. They would rather mount animals and fish or do anything other than stuff a duck. But they continue to take in birds to mount and their inventory grows. These individuals always can find something more interesting to do than mount that freezer full of ducks that has been without their attention for six months. A fellow taxidermist who comes in and shows quality bird mounts to the man with a freezer full of ducks may wind up quickly with six months' worth of bird mounting. The wholesale taxidermist may have to take less for his work than he normally would in his own shop for doing retail work. However, he will be working and making money when ordinarily he would be unemployed.

Quite a few taxidermists have low overhead and can mount specimens quickly, professionally, and for less money than other taxidermists while making a very good living in the wholesale taxidermy field. Some taxidermists prefer to do ducks and animals rather than fish. Here again, the wholesale fish taxidermist may find volumes of work by alleviating the problem of the taxidermist who has too much work.

The keys to making money in wholesale taxidermy are quite simple: First you have to be able to produce a quality product that the taxidermist you work for will be proud to give to his customers. You must be able to work quickly and get your specimens back to the taxidermist whose work you are subcontracting. Your employer has gotten behind with his work. He has allowed you to mount his specimens so he can get them back quicker to his customers. If it takes you as long to get the specimens back to him as it would have taken him to mount the specimens himself, you will not continue to get his business. The wholesale taxidermist must be careful not to work for more taxidermists than he can efficiently help. Also, do not let speed replace quality in your work.

I will never forget an incident several years ago when a young man came into my taxidermy business and began to discuss the possibilities of contracting the mounting of my turkeys.

"I've got one out in the car I mounted," he said. "Would you like to see it?"

Before I could answer the man was on his way out of my shop to bring in a sample of his work. When he returned he placed a mounted turkey on my office desk. I waited a long time before I spoke.

"Can I be honest with you?"

"Sure," the man answered.

"How many turkeys have you mounted before in your lifetime?"

"This is my second one," the proud young taxidermist grinned.

Next I asked, "How many turkey heads have you ever painted?"

"This is my first one," he told me.

If you specialize in one particular area of taxidermy, such as full-body mounts like these, you can offer your services to other taxidermists who may not feel confident in such jobs. You can also subcontract the work out, or refer the sportsman to another taxidermist and get a commission.

As nicely as I knew how I told the man that I thought before he attempted to contract turkey mounts from any other taxidermists in our area that he might spend a few more years learning how to mount and paint one.

Some folks may think me cruel. Yet the young man's work was so inferior to the quality required for commercial taxidermy that most taxidermists would have been far more brutal than me. Before you attempt to subcontract taxidermy work, be sure that you can mount commercial-grade specimens. You should be able to mount at least as well as the taxidermist whose work you are doing and in most cases your work should be superior to his. Plenty of money can be made in the wholesale taxidermy field if you have the quality and speed of mounting required to be successful.

The other side of the wholesale taxidermy market can be just as lucrative for the taxidermist who allows someone else to do the work that he cannot do. If you are a skilled fish mounter but lack the expertise in painting required to produce a high-quality fish mount, you may consider having another taxidermist paint your fish for a fee. If you prefer to mount fish and animals and really do not enjoy or feel that you are not competent to mount ducks, why not go ahead and take the ducks in, allow another specialist to do the actual mounting, and receive a portion of the profit for taking in the work? The medical profession applies this practice on a daily basis. When a doctor has a patient who has some type of complications the doctor is not as familiar with as a specialist may be, he calls in professional help and charges for it. The taxidermist can be just as professional. Rather than turning down work you do not feel competent to handle, why not take that work in, send it to a specialist, add a handling charge to his fee, and reap the benefits of having been able to mount the specimen your customer brought to you to be mounted? I have seen cases where taxidermists get a year or two behind in their work. Then, rather than hiring professional help to speed up their ability to mount these specimens, they lose business. Customers come to get their unmounted specimens and take them elsewhere or they move out of town or refuse to pay because the trophy has taken so long to be mounted.

Money definitely can be made on both sides of the wholesale taxidermy fence. Customers pay for quality work and quick service. The taxidermist who provides both will prosper. The ones who provide one or the other or neither will only make a small income.

(50) TAN THOSE SNAKESKINS. Snakeskin hatbands, vests, belts, and banjo straps really have come into style in the past few years and not without reason. The scales on a snake catch and reflect light and have beautiful colors and patterns that are very attractive if they are not gracing the back of a pit viper.

But there has been a problem in snakeskin tanning in recent years. The chemicals used to tan snakeskins sometimes will discolor the hides and cause the skins to appear washed out and faded. However, you can use a new process to tan snakeskins that protects the luster of the hide while still keeping the skin soft and flexible. This tanning process is relatively quick and inexpensive and will provide an excellent source of profit for the taxidermist looking for ways to make money in his spare time.

Skin the snake by splitting the hide on the belly side from the tip of the chin to the tip of the tail. I prefer to use a razor blade for this task. Be careful around the anus, as most snakes have a musk gland that, once opened, releases a foul smell that will get on your hands and create a problem. And be extremely careful around the head and the mount of pit vipers where the venom sacks are located. I have known sportsmen who received doses of poison from dead snakes.

After the hide is removed from the carcass, a small amount of skin and

Snakes can make lovely trophies and displays, from a full skin mount for wall showing and rattler belt buckles, to hatbands and other ideas. Proper tanning is the key to a good snakeskin job.

fat often will still be attached to the hide. Be careful in removing this excess tissue. A green snakeskin is very fragile and can tear if too much pressure is applied when removing the excess meat from the skin. Once the skin is cleaned of excess meat, it is ready to be soaked in a borax solution.

Add one handful of powdered borax to a gallon of water and stir until the borax is dissolved into the solution. Place your snakeskin into this solution and allow it to sit for one hour. The borax penetrates the skin and acts as a preservative. Next, take your snakeskin out of the solution and lightly scrape the borax solution off with clean water. Now the hide is ready to be stretched and a tanning solution applied. Be sure to tack your snakeskin to a board of greater width.

The inside of the skin should face up so the tanning solution can be applied. Do not put the tanning solution on the scale side of the hide. I prefer a ceiling tacker (hand staple gun) to tack the skin out rather than using hinges or nails, because I feel it stretches the skin more evenly.

The tanning solution is made of two parts denatured alcohol and one part glycerine. Mix these two ingredients thoroughly. Now take a soft-bristled paintbrush and paint the tanning solution onto the hide. A light coat will be sufficient. Stand the board with the snakeskin up so the excess tanning solution can drain off. Allow the skin to dry four to five hours, then apply another coat of the tanning solution. Three to five coats of the glycerine-alcohol mixture will be sufficient to preserve the skin while still allowing it to be pliable.

After the hide has dried for a week or more, cut around the edges of the staples to release the skin. Then you will have a clean, straight edge for your tanned skin rather than an edge full of holes and rust marks where the staples were. Many taxidermists will next attach the snakeskin to a piece of leather by using either contact cement or sewing the two edges of the snakeskin to it. In this way the snakeskin has more durability and will last longer than if it was not backed.

I have seen large Eastern diamondback rattlesnakes hides sewn together, then backed with material and made into beautiful vests for sportsmen. A large snakeskin may make several hatbands or belts, whereas a small one may only yield one.

Taxidermist Larry Blomquist says that he uses heavy strips of cardboard to back his hatbands:

> All I do is contact cement the snakeskin to the cardboard. Then I bend the cardboard to the desired length to fit around the crown of the hat and contact cement the two ends of the cardboard together. This makes a beautiful hatband and is also inexpensive to make. To make snakeskin belts, I prefer to use the belt kits that can be purchased from Tandy Leather Co., 9784 Pkwy. E, Birmingham, AL 35215. You can contact cement your snakeskin to the belt and use the holes that are already punched into the belt by the company to further secure the snakeskin to the leather by lacing the outer edges of the belt.
>
> Often a thin-skinned snake like a copperhead will lose its color when it has been tanned. To restore the color and make the snake look more life-like, I use either a red or orange stain on the belt blank. Then when I glue the snakeskin to the blank the stain shows through the skin and restores its

color. Also a rattlesnake skin may lose some of the yellow hue that is in the hide. So to restore this color, dye the belt yellow before you attach the snakeskin. Then the belt will have a more realistic, snakelike appearance. Remember in buying your belt blanks to buy the size blank that will most likely accommodate the skin that you have. It is better to have a portion of the skin wrap all the way around to the back side of the belt and be glued down than to have just enough skin to cover the front side. If you do not wrap the skin over the edge of the belt and lace the edge of the belt, the skin is more likely to come loose or the hide may more easily be torn.

Many sportsmen also request that a taxidermist make snakehides into small rugs similar to deer rugs. These rugs can be made by putting some type of batting or quilting material underneath the snakeskin, then sewing the hide to a piece of decorative felt. By adding small metal loops to the back of the rug, the skin will be suitable for a wall hanging that makes an interesting conversation piece in a sportsman's den. There are many different things that can be done with a properly tanned snakeskin, and this craft can be an excellent source of added revenue for the taxidermist who can find the snakes to tan.

(51) HOW TO MOUNT A TURKEY WITHOUT MOUNTING A TURKEY. One of the most unusual and attractive mounts I have ever seen is a turkey mount that does not involve an artificial body or the turkey's head or feet. I call this inexpensive, easy-to-do mount a skin mount.

To prepare the specimen for mounting, skin the turkey along the stomach like you normally would to mount him. Remove the head just above the beard, split the underside of the wings, and remove the meat from between the bones. Using Instant Mounting Fluid (available from Touchstone Taxidermy Supply, Rt. 1, Box 5294, Bossier City, LA 71111), inject the tail butt and the tips of the wings where a small amount of meat may remain. Using your knife, razor blade, or scissors, remove all excess meat or fat from the turkey's skin. Now rub powdered borax into the skin and into the cavity in each wing where the meat was removed.

Next, stretch the skin out, so the skin side is down and the feather side is up. Place a nail in the skin on either side of the back. From this base nail, run string to other nails around the edge of the wing so the string forces the feathers to lie down flat on the wing. Also place nails between each of the tail feathers that have been spread. By using a length of cord, go from one nail to the next making a loop around the nail so that the cord will hold the tail feathers down and in place.

Once the tail and wings are secured, allow the skin to dry in a warm, dry place for three to four weeks. While the turkey skin is drying, search the countryside for an old barn door or old barn wood that you can use to

So you don't want a full-body mount of your boss gobbler taking up precious space... but how about this treatment? You can readily visualize the size of the live bird with a wall flush mount. The first step shown here is to remove the skin from the bird and tack it out for drying while removing the meat from the wing bones.

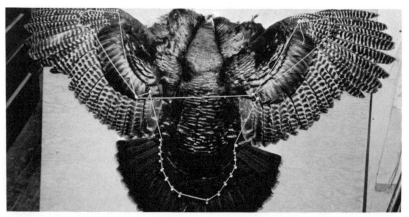

When the skin is secured to the board, drive nails into it as shown and wind heavy cord across the feathers and around the nails to hold the arrangement in place while it dries.

Once it's all dried, you can attach it by wires or hidden nails to a piece of barn board like this. Note that the beard is included. You could also include a photo or two of the hunt on the board, or a small metal plate with the date and other particulars of the successful trip.

mount the bird. Once the turkey skin is dried, use nails to attach the skin to the barn wood. Drive the nails through the skin and into the wood and use the feathers to hide the nail heads. Then no one will be able to tell how the hide has been attached. You can easily fashion a loop hanger with a length of clothesline so your turkey skin mount can be suspended from the wall. This mount will cost your customer far less than a full-bodied turkey mount and will make an attractive wall hanging for his den or office.

(52) TUMBLERS SAVE TIME. You can generate more income if you can produce more work in a given period of time. One of the most effective tools I have found to increase production is a barrel tumbler. This machine is composed of a drum that is turned by a small electric motor. Sawdust is placed inside the drum. Once the flesh has been removed and the specimen has been washed, a duck, deerskin, or other specimen can be thrown into the tumbler and the hair or feathers dried and polished by the rotating sawdust. Before we owned a tumbler we

A drum tumbler can save you hours of trying to fluff feathers and hair, and also polish the plumage and fur on your specimens and produce a higher-quality mount for you.

used blow dryers to dry specimens. Blow dryers are still effective tools. However, the sawdust tumbler not only dries but polishes and causes a sheen to appear on the specimens before you mount them. Time is saved by having the machinery, rather than the taxidermist, do the drying and polishing.

Different-sized drums are better for different specimens. For a bear skin, deer scalp, or moose skin, a 55-gallon drum may be your best tumbling device. For smaller animals like squirrels, foxes, bobcats, and birds, a smaller tumbler may be more advantageous. Besides the hardwood sawdust, six to two dozen tennis balls (depending on the size of the tumbler) should be placed inside the tumbler to aid in drying and polishing the specimens. Skins like fox, bobcat, and deer may tend to roll and wad up, but by adding the tennis balls the hides are lifted more and have a greater opportunity to be tumbled completely.

A clothes dryer with a broken heating element is an excellent, inexpensive tumbling machine. Since tumblers dry the skin, getting the skin to absorb dry preservative often is difficult. To counter this, spray the flesh side of the skin with denatured alcohol and allow the alcohol to penetrate the skin for 15 to 20 minutes. Then the skin will be moist and ready to accept the preservative. If you use water on the inside of the skin the preservative will dry, cake, and create lumps in your finished product. Using the tumbler can shave hours off the time you normally take to mount your specimens.

(53) TIPS FOR THE ESTABLISHED TAXIDERMIST. The taxidermist who has been in business for several years, yet does not seem to be able to produce quite enough money, has numerous alternatives to expand his business and at the same time decrease his overhead. One of the best ways to make more money in taxidermy is to spend less and keep more of the money you take in at your business.

Sometimes a taxidermist stays open too many hours for the volume of business he has. By reducing the number of hours your front office is open, you can turn off lights and heat and work in a small area in the back. Then you do not have the overhead of keeping showrooms and front offices open when there are no customers coming in to justify the expense.

Employees can greatly increase the amount of volume a taxidermist shop can produce, but they also weigh heavily on the expense side of the ledger. I have known taxidermists who kept employees on the payroll when there was no work for them to do. Also, some taxidermists do not work so that their employees will have a job. No one likes to terminate a good employee. But if your taxidermy business closes because you cannot generate enough income to keep the doors open, not only will that faithful employee be out of work but so will you. So look at what your employees are producing. In an eight-hour period some individuals will get out twice the work of their co-workers yet receive the same amount of pay. Soon that employee will wake up to the realization that, "I'm working twice as much but only receive the same pay as the fellow who is working half as hard as I am. So I'll lay back and take my time like he is doing."

Then when you, as an employer, try to speed your employees' work, they may come back with, "I can do it faster, but the quality of work I produce won't be nearly as good as if I take my time."

This is a problem, too. The taxidermist and his employees cannot produce more work without reducing quality. The only way to increase the output from the shop is to hire another employee who will work at the same rate as employees already on the payroll. I was caught in this dilemma a few years ago and realized that something had to change or my business would be in severe trouble. So I put my shop on a piecework basis. Employees became subcontractors. They were paid for performing certain tasks. I did not care how long it took them to perform the tasks, because I was only paying for services rendered rather than time expended. I would not accept unacceptable work, either.

Billy Ed was a good example of how the system worked. Billy Ed worked after college each day skinning out specimens, sewing up holes in hides, and preparing specimens for mounting. In an average five-day week, he took home $50.00 to $60.00 for his part-time work. When I changed from paying by the hour to subcontracting certain tasks, each previous employee became an independent businessman. Billy Ed could now work as little or as much as he wanted to work. He set his own hours. He knew at the end of each day how much he had made. The amount of pay he received at the end of each week was directly proportionate to the amount of work he had done in that week. The first week Billy Ed stepped into free enterprise as a private subcontractor he made $20.00 less than he had when he was an hourly employee. In the second week, he realized he could produce more and thereby earn more. So he made $10.00 more that week than he did as an hourly employee. Within eight weeks, Billy Ed doubled his salary and doubled the volume of work he could produce in the same amount of time he was working when I paid him by the hour. Even though my expenses had gone up, so had the volume of work that was produced in my shop. I increased the volume of work coming into the shop and expanded the business without additional employees. Billy Ed also expanded his business by producing more and thereby making more.

Often by rewarding employees with an incentive program, you increase the output of your shop without increasing the number of employees. I believe the only way to get maximum production and quality work in a taxidermy business is through a subcontractor-type relationship with your employees. Then the individuals who do good, quick work receive more compensation than do those who perform subquality work at a slower rate.

Most taxidermists fail to realize how much they are worth per hour. Many overestimate their worth while others fail to realize the value of their time. Unless you know the price that one hour of your time is worth, then you do not know how much to charge for specimens. You also do not know when you are making money and when you are not and how to budget your time so you make the maximum dollar for hours spent. The best way to determine this is to do three days of uninterrupted work. Hire someone to answer your phone, wait on customers, and do all the other things you do that will pull you away from your workbench. You may even have your help tell people who call and come by that you are on an extended research trip to develop new and better methods of mounting a specimen.

At the end of the three days, add up the total value of the work you have completed and divide that figure by the number of hours required to generate that much income. Now you know how much you are worth an hour. With this knowledge you can determine how long it takes you to mount a specimen and how much you should receive for your time. Next add in the cost of materials to mount that specimen, a 20 percent cost for overhead, and a 20 percent profit margin. You now have a figure that represents what your customers should pay for your services.

One of the biggest eye-openers I had about reducing overhead and increasing profits was when I considered how much money I was losing when I stopped work to run errands. If my time was worth $10.00 to $20.00 an hour and I was spending five to six hours a week running errands and getting supplies, then my material cost was $100.00 more each week than what I was figuring. By spending $100.00 worth of time getting supplies, I was making far less for my work than what I originally had assumed. I reasoned that if my time was worth $20.00 an hour, I could hire someone for $3.50 an hour to run errands while I spent my time mounting specimens. The additional employee meant another expense. However, the difference between $3.50 an hour and $20.00 an hour is $16.50. I would make $16.50 more if I stayed at my workbench and let someone else run the errands.

Knowing how much you are worth per hour is one of the most critical factors to be considered when trying to make more money in taxidermy. There may be some jobs that you will not be able to do so you will have the time to do the jobs that earn you more money.

Becoming a slave to the clock will yield big dividends. Being able to speed up your own productivity can increase greatly the amount of work you are able to turn out. Most of us feel we are self-disciplined when we accomplish the amount of work that we have set out to do each day. However, there is a higher discipline that is far more rewarding and satisfying and one that challenges our upper limit. Let me show you what I mean. Once I went into a taxidermy studio in Georgia and the conversation evolved into a discussion of fish skinning.

"How quickly can you skin a bass?" the taxidermist asked me.

"Well, I'm fairly quick," I replied. "But since I do more animals than fish, I'd say that my nephew, who is primarily a fish taxidermist, is faster than I am."

The man looked at me and grinned. "Well, there's not anybody in this area who can beat me," he said. "I can skin a fish in an hour and 15 minutes and have him ready to be mounted."

I hoped he would not ask how long it took Bubba to skin a fish to mount. But the inevitable question came out.

"Well, Bubba is pretty quick," I said, hoping to close the issue. But my answer spurred more questions.

"Well, how quick?" the man asked. "Do you think he is quicker than me?"

"Yessir, he is quicker than you are."

"Well, how quick?" the man kept asking.

"From the time you punch the button on a stopwatch until the bass hide is lying in the sink ready to be preserved and mounted, no more than five minutes will pass," I explained.

The man stood there in disbelief. Not until he saw the rapid hands, scissors, and knives of Bubba would he believe it, but William Archie Phillips III (Bubba) was skinning bass when most children were playing with Tinker Toys. Each time he got quicker. His daddy first gave him a lollipop, then a dime, then a quarter, then a dollar and when he broke 10 minutes per fish, he got a $20.00 bonus. Bubba just wanted to find out what his upper limits were. So he set a clock in front of his workbench and began to race it each day until he became a free man by breaking the five minute mark. His daddy used to say, "Son we've got to stay here at work tonight until we get all these fish done—no matter how long it takes."

There might be 10 or 15 fish in the sink to be skinned. In less than two hours, Bubba would be watching television, whereas many other taxidermists would have to burn the late midnight oil. Some taxidermists want to equate speed with lack of quality work, but just the opposite is true. A fast taxidermist will make every stroke of his knife, every swipe of his brush, and every move with his modeling tool count. As his skill develops, so will his speed. Often the faster a taxidermist is, the more skill he can demonstrate on certain tasks.

Billy Ed is another illustration of that principle. Billy Ed's normal time for skinning out a deerhead, cutting out the horns, putting the scalp in the freezer, and taking the horns upstairs was 30 to 45 minutes. When he became an independent subcontractor, his time dropped from 45 minutes to five minutes for the same task. Once again, Billy Ed allowed the clock to become his taskmaster. Each day he would race the clock to shave seconds off his time. And each day he became more proficient, more skilled, and a more valuable employee.

The taxidermist who wants to make more money should have a bigger clock and learn to depend more heavily on it. Big Ben is your friend, not your enemy. By making you move faster, he will teach you how to get more done in a shorter period of time. He will teach you to be able to handle large volumes of work on opening days in normal working hours without having to stay up all night. He will make you more money than any other gimmick, gadget, or technique you will learn. He is not an evil taskmaster, because he will buy more free time for you than you ever have had before. Jobs that once took three and four hours to complete can be reduced to two hours to give you the time for more recreational activities or more work—whichever you choose.

(54) THE TAXIDERMIST AS A SALESMAN. Often all that is required to have more specimens to mount is for the taxidermist to take the time to sell his customer more than one mount. The classic example is the sportsman who brings a deerhead in with the hide and feet attached.

"I just want to get a shoulder mount," the sportsman may say. And if the taxidermist does not take the time to sell the customer more than a shoulder mount, that probably will be all the business he receives from the man that day.

But as a salesman my next question is, "What do you plan to do with the feet?"

And the customer will answer usually, "Throw them away, I guess."

Now I have the chance to show him deer-foot gun racks, deer-foot thermometers, deer-foot lamps, deer-foot hat racks, and even a deer-foot knife handle. If nothing else, I will volunteer to cut the toenails off the deer's feet and make a handsome deer-foot necklace for the sportsman's wife or girlfriend for a small fee.

Then, as I start to cut the scalp away from the hide, I may comment on what a beautiful hide this particular deer head has and how nice it would be tanned for a rug. If the customer does not bite at this suggestion, I will come back with, "You could have the hide made into deerskin driving gloves or dress gloves for your wife."

If the sportsman still does not react, I suggest having the hide tanned with the hair off so he can use the leather to make knife sheaths or change purses. At the very least, we will be able to cut the deer's tail off, skin it out, and preserve it for $5.00 so he can use the hair for tying fishing jigs.

Often our customers do not give a taxidermist more business because they are unaware of the options they have when they bring specimens to be mounted. When a sportsman wants a duck mounted, we also can ask if he wants a habitat mount that includes dried shrubs and wildflowers so

Keep a quality coonskin cap in your shop where customers can easily spot it. Their queries can lead to more sales, even when they come into the place on other business.

his duck is in a more lifelike setting. Always have some of this work on display; many times the customer will choose the added option. Then I say, "I guess you want a nameplate on the mount with your name, the date you killed it, and the place," to which the customer will often answer in the affirmative. Once again I have added dollars to my business.

Beaver hats are ideal for sportsmen simply because they keep heads warm and look good at the same time.

Even when a customer comes in and wants a deer-foot gun rack, I can receive extra money and provide an added feature for his trophy by suggesting, "You can put a mirror in the middle of those deer feet and really have an attractive piece of furniture as well as a gun rack."

By selling more to the same number of people who frequent your shop, you actually can increase the amount of money you take in during the course of a season. The taxidermist who is an artist only and never develops his sales skill always will have to be satisfied with less than his potential from his chosen profession. But by learning how to sell and continuing to sell, you can add more work to an existing business.

(55) DEERSKIN GLOVES. Deerskins have very little value when sold on the fur market. Deerskin products, however, are often quite expensive. One of the easiest products to sell is deerskin gloves. Buckskin makes excellent driving gloves and beautiful dress gloves. The taxidermist can take many of the hides that he ordinarily would throw away, flesh and salt them, and have them made into some of these fine leather gloves at a relatively low cost.

If you choose not to tie your money up in gloves for display, the W.D. Place Co., Hwy. 60 W, Hartford, WI 53027 has an excellent exchange program. For each deerskin you send fleshed and salted with tail and neck included, the Place Co. will send you one pair of deerskin gloves free of charge.

Many times a sportsman will bring in a deer head with cape, feet, and head attached. He may want only a horn mount, so all of the hide will have to be thrown away. However, by fleshing and salting that same hide and shipping it to the Place Co., you will receive a nice pair of deerskin gloves instead of adding weight for the garbage collectors. Once you acquire gloves for display, you may want to take orders for custom-made gloves, save deerskins, ship the orders and the hides to the Place Co., and sell your customers excellent hand warmers. Deerskin can add another dimension to your taxidermy business and let you make money from discarded hides.

(56) EVERY YEAR I GET FIVE TO TEN CALLS FOR COONSKIN HATS. The reasons vary widely. One may be a small boy wanting a hat to dress up in for a play, or one of the new breed of mountain men may need a coonskin cap to complete his outfit. If it is not coonskin hats the outdoorsmen are hunting, it is fox skin hats, skunk hats, coyote hats, or badger hats. Certain people want hats made from animal pelts.

One of the oldest hat makers is Fortman Bros., N. Rt. 668, Rt. 1, Box 213, St. Mary's, OH 45885. You can buy coonskin hats for $40.50 to $69.00 depending on the quality of fur from which the hats are made. You can save $10.00 to $15.00 per hat by sending in the raw skin to have the hat made.

Another type of hat that once was common and has experienced a revival in the past few years is the beaver hat. You can order these from Beca Furs, Rt. 1, Box 2, Sturgis, MS 39769. These beaver trooper hats come in two styles: the solid beaver hat and the beaver hat with the suede crown. The hats are warm, stylish, and will provide another product for you to offer your customers.

(57) SELL MOUNTING KITS. Some people want to mount their own specimens. Just like the decoy carvers and painters who could probably hire a craftsman to carve and paint much more beautiful decoys than they can fashion themselves, these people want the satisfaction of having mounted a specimen they have taken. The quality of workmanship is not nearly as critical to these outdoorsmen as the knowledge that they have done it themselves. These individuals will provide some extra dollars to the taxidermist who can meet their needs.

Larry Blomquist sells mounting kits. He describes them as follows:

> I always keep more squirrel forms and duck forms than I need for the specimens I have to mount. So when someone comes in and tells me that they want to mount their own duck or squirrel, I sell them the mounting kit. With a squirrel this includes the form, the eyes, the wires and the preservatives they will need to mount the squirrel, along with a needle and thread. The same type of supplies are provided in my duck-mounting kit. Then the next thing they usually will want is some type of driftwood to mount their critter on. So I sell them a piece of driftwood too. I have found that by providing kits for sportsmen, I can increase the amount of money I take in and I also pick up new customers like this. If the customer takes a real trophy he will bring it to me for a professional mounting job. In the meantime if he has a specimen he simply wants to mount for the fun of it he will buy his supplies from me. So by meeting his needs I am able to serve him in two ways and able to earn money from two different sources from the same customer.

(58) EASY PAYMENT PLAN. One of the ways to make more money in taxidermy is to make your service more affordable to more people. To do this often you have to be able to work with your customers on some type of payment program. I once had a man who wanted to have a deer head mounted but he did not have the money and was out of work.

"I can pay you $5.00 every two weeks until I pay the deer head off," the man told me.

Knowing of his lack of funds and realizing the man was sincere, I agreed to hold the deerhead in my freezer until he paid off his 50 percent deposit. Then when his deposit was paid I would mount the head and he could pick it up when he completed his payments.

Every two weeks the man came by and laid a crisp $5.00 bill in my hand.

"Don't worry, Mr. Phillips. I'll get that deer head paid off yet," he would say to me.

And sure enough, within six months he had paid off his deer head. I not only received compensation for my work and added a new customer to my business, I also made a friend who brought other business into my shop.

LARRY BLOMQUIST TAXIDERMY
803 E. Morris St. • P.O. Box 2945
Hammond, La. 70404

PAYMENT PLAN

Name: _____

Address: _____

City_____ St._____ Zip_____

Phone: _____

Trophy_____ Date Received_____

Cost	$_____	
Deposit	$_____	
Balance	$_____	
Service Charge	$_____	
Total Balance	$_____	

SERVICE CHARGES:

$ 50 - $100	$2.00
101 - 150	3.00
151 - 200	4.00
201 - 250	5.00
251 - 500	6.00

PAYMENT RECORD		
DATE	CREDIT	DEBIT

Number of payments: _____ @ _____ each

Balance, if any, after payments are completed $_____.
(Balance due upon completion of mount)

Date of first payment: _____

Date of last payment: _____

I understand and agree to the above payment plan.

_____
Customer Signature

LARRY BLOMQUIST TAXIDERMY PAYMENT PLAN

Total amount of payments: $_____

Number of payments: _____ @ $_____ each

Balance, if any, after payments are completed: $_____
(Balance due upon completion of mount)
Please use the payment cards below

4

· PAYMENT CARD ·
(Please send with payment)
P.O. Box 2945•Hammond, La. 70404

Bal. before payment: _____

Amount of payment:_____

Date Due: _____

Name: _____

Trophy:_____ Trophy #_____

5

· PAYMENT CARD ·
(Please send with payment)
P.O. Box 2945•Hammond, La. 70404

Bal. before payment: _____

Amount of payment: _____

Date Due: _____

Name: _____

Trophy:_____ Trophy #_____

6

· PAYMENT CARD ·
(Please send with payment)
P.O. Box 2945•Hammond, La. 70404

Bal. before payment: _____

Amount of payment:_____

Date Due: _____

Name: _____

Trophy:_____ Trophy #_____

1

· PAYMENT CARD ·
(Please send with payment)
P.O. Box 2945•Hammond, La. 70404

Bal. before payment: _____

Amount of payment:_____

Date Due: _____

Name: _____

Trophy:_____ Trophy #_____

2

· PAYMENT CARD ·
(Please send with payment)
P.O. Box 2945•Hammond, La. 70404

Bal. before payment: _____

Amount of payment:_____

Date Due: _____

Name: _____

Trophy:_____ Trophy #_____

3

· PAYMENT CARD ·
(Please send with payment)
P.O. Box 2945•Hammond, La. 70404

Bal. before payment: _____

Amount of payment:_____

Date Due: _____

Name: _____

Trophy:_____ Trophy #_____

Keep your records straight and offer a payment plan for your customers with a form such as this. It makes things easier for both of you. If your business is really expanding, you might consider buying a personal home computer to handle the record-keeping.

A taxidermist friend of mine has developed an easy payment plan for his customers. He has payment cards printed on white perforated cardboard. The customers can pay for their work in either four- or six-month installments. With each payment card, this enterprising taxidermist also gives his customers four or six self-addressed envelopes to mail the payment card and their money in each month. Since many people are used to time payment plans for everything from automobiles to furniture, this system works well in most budgets and has provided a method by which customers who think they do not have the money can afford to have their trophies mounted. By making your work more affordable through the use of a time payment system, especially during economically hard times, you can in fact make your service more affordable to more people and thereby increase the volume of work you receive.

(59) MORE BUCKS IN BIG BUCK CONTESTS. One of the best sales techniques in the world today is the "something for nothing" concept. Most recently we have seen this philosophy applied with slogans like "Buy one, get one free," "Two for the price of one," factory rebates, and so on. The "something for nothing" philosophy does motivate people to action and helps bring work into your business.

There are two ways a taxidermist can offer "something for nothing" and bring in additional business, and both methods are tied to big buck and big bass contests. Many taxidermists offer prizes for the largest deer or the largest fish brought into their shops to be mounted in a season. Another system is to put all your customers' names in a hat and have a drawing at the end of each season for a prize. An added feature to a big buck contest that will generate traffic in your shop and create a lot of excitement in your region is to use some type of bulletin board to post the top 10 standings for fish or deer brought into your shop during the season. Another tool that creates a lot of traffic is to keep a scrapbook with photos of each customer's specimen, their name, address, the date they brought it in, and what it scored.

A typical big buck contest may be run like this. All the deer to be considered for the contest will be measured using the Boone and Crockett scoring system. There are two categories—one for typical racks and the other for non-typical racks. There is also a youth division for hunters 15 years old or under with prizes awarded for first, second, and third place in both categories of racks. In the same contest, everyone who brings a deer head in for mounting will be eligible for a drawing of a nice prize like a shotgun, a free mount, and so on. So a customer has four chances of winning. He can win a prize for either first, second, or third place in his division, or he can win a prize for simply bringing his deer head into your shop to be mounted. Anyone who brings a deer head in to be mounted has an opportunity to get "something for nothing."

Also, the biggest deer heads in your area will find their way to your shop from the hunters wanting to compete for the prize awarded the largest head. One taxidermist living in Louisiana close to the Mississippi line added yet another twist to the contest. He awards a prize for the most typical and non-typical deer killed in Louisiana by one man, the biggest typical and non-typical deer killed in Mississippi, and the biggest typical and non-typical deer killed in all other states. By offering more prizes he induces hunters to bring their work to him.

The same philosophy will work during the spring and summer with a big bass or trophy trout program. The biggest fish of the month can win for the angler a free mount and/or merchandise or cash. Then, at the end of the fishing season, a large trophy can be awarded for the biggest fish caught for the season. Sportsmen, just like everyone else in our society, are contest and prize oriented. They are all looking for that "something for nothing" reward when they take a big fish or big deer. The taxidermist who adds the prize incentive for sportsmen to bring trophies into his shop increases his sales volume.

The key to success in a prize program is to make sure the value of the prize offered is large enough to draw the sportsmen. Often you can purchase prizes at a reduced rate by offering to promote the sporting goods dealer and/or manufacturer who lets you have the prize at a reduced rate or at no cost. Many times you may be able to trade taxidermy work for hunting or fishing equipment with the local sporting dealer or manufacturer. One taxidermist I know of gives away a handmade knife as part of the prize package for the sportsman taking the biggest deer of the season. The knife is on display in the taxidermy shop throughout the season. In the display with the knife is the knife maker's name, address, and telephone number with the retail cost of the knife. All the advertising and promotional materials that are sent out to customers also carry information about the knife and the maker. So the knife maker receives a large amount of publicity and promotion of his product for the cost of a knife. You may be able to work with other manufacturers in the same way. Contests may be the key to more big bucks in your business.

(60) SHOW STOPPERS. A taxidermist with a little imagination and creativity can be worth thousands of dollars to a company with a product to sell. The classic example of this was at a Shooting, Hunting, Outdoor Trade Show (SHOT Show) sponsored by the National Shooting Sports Foundation.

Walking along an aisle that was parallel to eight or 10 other aisles, I caught a glimpse of a whole deer hanging upside down on the edge of one of the booths. I took five more steps and began to wonder if I really saw what I thought I saw. So I walked back, looked again, and sure enough—there was a **200**-pound whitetail buck hanging by his hocks, upside down, ready to be field dressed. Once I had assured myself that I

A show-stopper or just plain eye-grabber can lure potential customers to your shop. This hanging-deer mount, a happy sight for deer hunters, added business for this company, selling dressing kits at an outdoor trade show.

had seen a large buck deer ready for skinning hanging in the middle of the Dallas, Texas, Convention Center, I started to walk away. About three aisles over, my mind went back to the buck. I wondered how in the world they were going to keep that deer from stinking for four days while the show was running.

"The buck has got to be frozen," I told myself. "They've got to put him in the freezer every night after the show to get him hard enough to keep him from smelling during the day."

Yes, that had to be the solution. I went back to see the deer again. The hair was not wet, and from a distance the deer did not appear to be frozen. So I left to tour the show and see the other exhibits. But that upside-down buck continued to plague my mind. How had the company done it? I knew the deer could not be mounted because there is no form for mounting a deer hanging upside down. Obviously it was not a mount.

"I can't believe the health department is letting them get away with having a whole deer hanging in a trade show," I kept thinking.

Finally, when I could stand it no longer, I went for a closer examination of the upside-down deer. The deer was, in fact, mounted. Some taxidermist had spent a lot of time modifying a form and sewing, very meticulously, so that his seams were almost invisible. The reason the deer was hanging upside down was that the WALPRO Co. was selling a deer butchering kit which included a small, lightweight block and tackle, a meat gambrel, a saw, and a meat bag for completely butchering the deer. All this equipment fit together nicely in a small carrying case that the sportsman could take with him into the field.

Although the product was good, laying on a table it would appear just like some other gadget that nobody could figure out how to use. Even if an outdoorsman knew what it was, nobody would really be impressed with a deer-butchering kit. But once you saw that deer hanging upside down in the middle of the biggest hunting and shooting show in the nation, you had to stop, investigate, and look at the WALPRO product.

Not only could potential buyers understand how the butchering kit worked, they could actually see a deer being hung by it. Without the mounted deer—a show stopper—the product would have been just another kit, receiving little attention from the media or the buyers. But thousands of people like myself walked past WALPRO's booth, were attracted by the deer, came in, and heard the story about the product. The sales of this mail-order product at that show mushroomed into an international business with buyers from Sweden, Canada, and France as well as across the United States all eager to purchase the complete deer butchering kit. There were even requests for similar products to be made to skin elk and bear.

The WALPRO kit may have sold well on its own, but there is no question about it—the upside-down deer brought in thousands of customers who would have walked right by this booth without a second glance. That type of creativity by a taxidermist can put thousands of dollars into a manufacturer's hands. And lest you think that upside-down deer are the only creative, innovative adaptations from the taxidermy trade in the marketing of new outdoor products, how about giant bass?

I am addicted to sports shows and outdoor shows, for I believe they often hold keys and ideas for an enterprising taxidermist. At a boat show a few years ago I was browsing the many booths and exhibitions when high atop a display case I spied an enormous largemouth bass. The fish had to weigh 50 or 60 pounds. Because of my experience in the outdoor field, I knew that there was no way that bass could be a bass. So I walked on past it. But then I wondered. How in the world had the people gotten such an exact replica of a largemouth? I looked at the fish from two aisles away and was struck by how lifelike the giant bass appeared. Finally, curiosity got the best of me. I went over to the booth and began to study the 50-pound bass. The first thing I realized was that the fish was not a fiberglass reproduction. The scale detail was too exact and the fins were too thin to have been a fiberglass reproduction. The teeth on the inside of the mouth were real also, and it was apparent that the fish, whatever it was, was a real fish. The structure of the body, the placement of the fins, everything about the fish gave the appearance of a tremendous largemouth. But it could not be a largemouth.

"There are no 50-pound largemouths," I told myself. And if there were, the catch and the fisherman would have been written up in every major magazine in the country.

But how had some taxidermist mounted such an exquisite specimen of a largemouth that did not exist? Close examination and questioning revealed the answer. It was a jewfish (*Epinephelus itajara*) or a saltwater grouper, which is fairly common in southern Florida and throughout the tropical American Atlantic. The fish had been well mounted and then painted using the same color patterns as a freshwater largemouth bass. The gill covers, which are normally more pointed than a bass', had been trimmed to give the appearance of the oval gill covers of the largemouth. The tail also had been shaped to resemble that of a largemouth bass. The taxidermist had been skillful. Except for these two modifications and the paint job, the fish was a largemouth bass to all who saw it. Needless to say, the mount attracted many sportsmen into the fishing tackle dealer's booth, not to see his products but to discuss the giant bass. Once the sportsmen were captured in his booth and the giant bass was discussed, salesmen had the opportunity to show their wares and sell their products. Whether or not show goers believed the giant fish was a largemouth or not was irrelevant. They stopped, looked, and came into the booth.

Unusual attention getters always have drawn a crowd and always will draw a crowd. But upside-down deer and 50-pound bass are not the only markets for the taxidermist in search of more income in the sporting goods market. Display taxidermy can be rented out to manufacturers to use in their booths to help sell products.

A giant elk, a massive moose, or an extremely large deer head will pull passersby into a booth. A large array of mounted fish or big fish also will stop a crowd. Ducks and geese, mounted with creative flair, will cause some to stop and inquire. For manufacturers or stores who have something to sell to sportsmen, a taxidermy display or piece of unusual taxidermy work that they have purchased can add thousands of dollars to their businesses. For more ideas along these same lines, take every opportunity to visit outdoor shows. Notice what draws attention and what you have or can mount to serve as an attention getter. Once again, creativity, imagination, style, and flamboyance often will bring more money into your taxidermy business.

Another way to utilize show stoppers is to rent space in a boat show or outdoor show yourself to promote your taxidermy business. One of the keys to bringing more business in is to know more people. The more people you know and the more folks who know you and your work, the more salesmen you have in the field promoting and advertising your taxidermy business. And many taxidermists have found that one of the best ways to display their work, meet more customers, and sell some of the items they have created is working an outdoor show. You can display a quantity of your work and cause more people to stop and inquire by having a large space at the show. However, a large space is not a necessity. A small booth with large and unusual specimens will stop visitors to a show and draw them into your booth to talk hunting and fishing and discuss taxidermy work.

To display more work in less space, use a photo album. Joel Stone, a taxidermist in Birmingham, Alabama, does an excellent job of showing a great number of specimens through the use of photo albums in his booth. The color pictures show various specimens of game heads, birds, and animals in different mounted positions. When a passerby inquires if Stone can mount a duck in a landing position, he may not have the waterfowl on the wall, but you can bet there are at least one to three pictures of mounted ducks lighting in his photo album.

The one-on-one contact with the sportsman that the taxidermist has at an outdoor show can pay great dividends. There are several items that you should have with you in the booth at a sports show:

1. Business Cards. Anyone you talk with or who inquires about your work should not leave your booth without at least one of your business cards.

2. Posters. When a sportsman says, "I'm in a hunting club or a fishing club in the southern end of the state," the taxidermist should reply, "Would you mind putting up one of my posters at your club?" I have found that most outdoorsmen will put up the posters, especially if the poster features an attractive game head, bird, or fish.

3. Price Lists. Give price lists to sportsmen who inquire about the costs of various specimens.

4. Pen and Notebook. Write down the names, addresses, and telephone numbers of people who mention they have a specimen in the freezer that they may try to get to you in the next week or two. Often you can rekindle their interest in having their specimen mounted and refresh their memory of seeing your work at the show by giving these interested sportsmen a call a week or so after the show. Also, sometimes passersby will mention that they belong to a civic club or sporting group that invites speakers to discuss outdoor topics. Once again, take their names and addresses and give them a call after the show.

5. Something to Sell. Most of the time a taxidermist can recover the cost of his booth and make a profit by having outdoor products available for sale at these shows. Earrings, necklaces, hats, and many of the other products that we have mentioned in the book can be sold at an outdoor show so that the taxidermist not only does his promotional work at the show but adds dollars and income while he is doing it.

One common question to listen for is, "Can you do this, that, or the other?" Sportsmen are always wanting something different or unusual made from wildlife trophies or wildlife by-products. The enterprising taxidermist always will answer this question in the affirmative. Once you have the job you can determine at a later date how you are going to perform this work. Making the sale always precedes producing the product.

Dozens of other ways can be used to generate income at an outdoor show, so be creative and look for opportunities that can and will present themselves when you meet the public.

(61) JACKALOPES, UNICORNS, THING-A-MA-JIGS, AND WHAT-CHA-MA-CALLITS. There are several schools of thought on taxidermy. The most prevalent thinking is that the taxidermist is like an artist who plies his trade to recapture lifelike appearances in fish and wildlife. Great attention is paid to detail so it appears that the animal just stepped out of the woods or the fish just swam under a large rock. Carried to an extreme this school of thought would have little place for thing-a-ma-jigs and whatcha-ma-callits, let alone jackalopes and unicorns.

Then there is another school of thought. People who adopt this philosophy believe that taxidermy is fun and that their ability to create and produce quality work and different and unusual specimens is only limited by their imagination. So they produce unique and unusual oddities in their spare time for fun and profit. Probably the most widely publicized is the jackalope—a rabbit (either cottontail, swamp, or jackrabbit) whose head has been mounted with antlers sprouting from the skull. These antlers may be purchased from many of the taxidermy supply houses. If a jackalope is in your future, Taxidermy Supply Co., Rt. 1, Bossier City, LA 71010 has an excellent book entitled *Rabbit and Jackalope Heads Mounted in One Hour Without Sewing*. The book costs only $2.00 and gives complete instructions on the "how-to" of jackalope mounting. Taxidermy Supply Co. also sells complete jackalope kits— without antelope horns—or six-point deer antlers that fit the kits.

The taxidermist who mounts jackalopes can invent all kinds of wild tales about where they come from, what they do, and why they are not commonly found in his region and really have a good time telling a story of the animal heads he created. The jackalope is also an excellent trophy to be presented as a gag gift at a deer hunting club. I have been in meetings before where the president of the club stands up and gives all the credentials of either the most successful hunter in the group or the most unsuccessful hunter. In either case at the end of the ceremony, he says something like, "And we have here tonight the mounted head of the largest buck this hunter ever took. After wounding the animal, old Joe Doe had to get down on his hands and knees and crawl into a briar patch, armed only with his knife to face the fierce charge and slashing horns of this awesome buck. But though scarred and bleeding, gored and bruised, Joe Doe would not give up the fight. Finally he subdued this buck and we have the head here to present to him tonight."

Old Joe will get up from his chair, walk to the front of the room and there be presented with an outstanding jackalope mount, created by a taxidermist with a sense of humor.

Another excellent mount, if you live in an area that has both coons and armadillos, is to mount a coon with an armadillo shell on its back. This apparition will create all kinds of interest and comments from coon hunters and makes an excellent mount to be given to a crusty old coon hunter who has chased one particular coon for many years without catching him.

Some taxidermists may believe jackalopes to be an invention of some midwest taxidermist's imagination, but such is not the case. The jackalope was conceived in the castles of European noblemen. A skilled taxidermist took bird heads, animal bodies, and fish fins to create weird creatures. These creatures were supposed to be gnomes, trolls, and all

THIS JACK-O-LOPE WAS STALKED &
KILLED BY J. S. KEITH ON HIS
SAFARI 1-11-78 INTO THE JUNGLE
OF GUNOLA. A WINCHESTER 458.

MAGNUM WAS USED AND
WAS DOWNED WITH
ONLY THREE
SHOTS.

Maybe you don't have a trophy from your summer camp snipe-hunting days, but you can recall the charge of a rogue jack-e-lope with a mount like this. Novelty items are ready sellers and can increase your profits with a minimum of effort.

kinds of mythical, magical creatures. They adorned castle walls much like the mounted trophies do today.

The fabled unicorn may have been perpetuated and kept alive by the creativity and skill of a medieval taxidermist. Even today unicorns can be created by thinking taxidermists. A horn growing out of the center of a

If you don't think the jack-e-lope story will impress your hunting pals, you should get their interest with the unicorn, or uni-whatever, that circled your campfire. A few of these items in your shop should bring added sales.

fox's head or a duck's bill or in the middle of a goat's head will give rise to all kinds of stories. Bird wings on the backs of minks and squirrels make interesting mounts. But I guess everyone's favorite is the duck head inside the turtle shell with strange looking feet coming out the side. This is a good critter to give duck hunters who are notorious for shooting waterfowl on the water but are unable to kill them.

Using animal parts to create new and unusual mountings will only be limited by the taxidermist's imagination. The jackalopes, unicorns, thing-a-ma-jigs, and whatcha-ma-callits will provide a lucrative market for the taxidermist with creativity who is interested in mounting one-of-a-kind specimens.

(62) UNUSUAL HEAD MOUNTS. When the term *head mount* is used, most sportsmen think of game heads. However, some unusual head mounts make excellent novelty gifts and attractive trophies for the sportsman who does not have room or does not desire to have the whole critter mounted.

Some typical examples are turkey head mounts, where the head of the turkey is mounted on a small plaque and the name of the hunter, the date the turkey was taken, and any other pertinent information is attached to the plaque. Another beautiful head mount is that of a duck. The head of a wood duck, mallard, widgeon, or teal can be attached to a small panel and make an interesting mount for the sportsman. Beautifully colored and with tricolored eyes, the pheasant is probably one of the most attractive bird heads that can be mounted.

Once again, a taxidermist is limited only by his imagination and creativity. A crow's head mounted on a panel may make an excellent gag gift for the old crow in the office. Or a rooster's head can be mounted and presented to a man who thinks he is the cock of the walk.

Years ago the head mounting of fish was a popular form of taxidermy. In my area largemouth bass and smallmouth bass were the primary species used in head mounts. Mounting a big bass' head is relatively inexpensive and can preserve the trophy for the sportsman with a nameplate recording the date and place of the catch.

But around our home, as people became more affluent, mounting the big bass' head gave way to full-body mounts. However, there is still a volume of business waiting for the taxidermist who promotes head mounting of fish, which requires little time and expertise but can and will add needed dollars to the business. And, in the same way, a large saltwater billfish will command a very high price, whereas a quarter mount of the head and bill of that same fish will preserve the trophy for the customer at a lesser price.

One of the best ways to introduce head mounts into your business is to offer the head mount as a substitute when you have a customer who balks at paying to have a whole-body fish mount. Although you may not receive as much money for doing a head mount as you would a fully-body mount, you will be paid some money and perform a service for a customer who may come back later with more work.

Do not overlook the head mount. Offer these as alternatives for customers who would leave your business without having their fish mounted or to add larger profits to your business.

(63) PETS—DOLLARS OR PROBLEMS? There are big dollars in mounting pooches and other pets, but there are also some cautions. I knowingly have mounted only two pets in my taxidermy career. There is a very good reason for this. A pet differs from a wild animal in that it has developed an intimate relationship with its owner. That pet has a certain expression, mannerism, and way of looking at its owner that never can be recaptured with all the skill and expertise of the taxidermist. The pet will look always like something stuffed to its owner. For that reason, I always decline mounting pets even though the dollars that can be charged for this service can be extremely high. The two exceptions I referred to earlier were a dog that was tanned and a pigeon that was mounted.

"Do you do tanning?" the lady on the other end of the phone asked.

"Yes, we do," I replied.

"Well, I have the skin of my dog that I would like to have tanned," the female caller said in broken English to my amazement.

After I went through my explanation as to why we did not mount pets, let alone tan their hides, the Japanese lady was quick to explain.

"In my country these dogs are held in such high esteem that any master owning such a dog is bound by tradition and honor to have the skin of the dog tanned," she said. "This is an honorable custom, and one that my family has practiced for centuries. I would like to perpetuate this custom in this country."

After some more discussion the lady convinced me to have the hide of her pet pooch tanned. The animal had already been skinned and salted. I shipped the hide to the tannery. Once the dog pelt was returned I notified my customer. She was well pleased with the skin.

Old Pete was a 13-year-old pigeon that had been part of a family since the time he fell out of a nest as a small bird. Pete's owner spent hours convincing me to mount the pigeon. For some reason I agreed and the pigeon was preserved. Pete's owner was pleased, and I was glad the job was over.

But for each of these satisfied customers, many more would not have been. And so I have chosen not to mount pets.

Some taxidermists freeze-dry pets for their customers. This, too, seems a bit morbid to me and does not provide the lifelike replicas I feel most clients want in their specimens. Although there is good money in mounting pets and although quite a few taxidermists who expand their income by performing this service for bereaved owners, I have chosen not to be a mortician of loved ones. You may feel differently.

(64) THROUGH-THE-WALL MOUNTS. Many sportsmen with dens or trophy rooms are looking for something new, different, or unusual to be placed in these areas. With the new life-size urethane forms, taxidermists can stand ready and willing to offer their customers unique mounts. Almost any form can be cut in half, and almost any critter can be displayed by putting half the animal on one side of the wall in one room while the other half is displayed on the other side of the wall in the next room. Lions can be seen jumping through walls, a big buck may have his hindquarters on one side of the partition while his head and front legs protrude from the other side, or a fox may be seen jumping through a wall. There is no limit to the creative half-mounts that can be used to make interesting illusions for your customers.

And forms can be bought from taxidermy supply houses of coons inside of logs or half foxes crawling out of logs. Forms can be modified and changed to create a variety of mounts that will interest and satisfy customers.

(65) TEACHING BEGINNERS AND BUYING FROM VETERANS. Most taxidermists try to discourage beginners in the field, and the reason is quite simple. These beginners often will become competitors, and that competition will slice into the profit pie of an established taxidermist. However, the beginner will learn the craft and will buy his supplies from someone. The volume of materials he will purchase may not be high, but the profit margin may be large enough to justify selling to him.

Teaching beginners in your shop also may be an area of income to be considered. But criteria should be set before you agree to sell your knowledge to a potential competitor:

1. Where does the potential student plan to set up his shop? How close his business will be to yours will have a bearing on whether or not you will teach him.
2. Is the student willing to come the required number of hours to perfect his talents in the craft of taxidermy?
3. Is the student willing to pay a substantial price to justify the time taken away from your business to train him?

One of the traps I have seen taxidermists fall into is to take in a student who says, "I'll work for nothing just so I can learn."

The student is not working for nothing. He is taking up your time and your space to learn his trade. The amount of time and materials you expend in training him will not equal the "free" labor he gives for your services and knowledge.

A good yardstick to use in determining how much to charge a student for instruction is as follows:

1. How much could you earn per day mounting specimens?
2. If the student lives close by, how many specimens per year do you think he will take from your business?
3. Will you be able to perform any other work while training this student?
4. Can you train more than one student at a time?
5. How much have the skills and knowledge you possess cost you to attain?

A student can take a mail-order taxidermy course or purchase a book to learn taxidermy. However, if that student wants first-hand experience under the guidance and supervision of a qualified taxidermist, he should be willing to pay the price that you determine is just and fair for your skills.

The buying and selling of knowledge can increase your ability to earn money in taxidermy. Let me explain. With the beginner, you are selling your "brain" and its information, skill, and knowledge to someone for a profit. By the same token, you can make money by buying the "brains" of other taxidermists.

If you know a taxidermist with a speciality in mounting that makes his work better, more unusual, or different from yours and you want to learn how he does what he does, offer to pay for this knowledge. Although I believe that a large amount of information can be gleaned at seminars and conferences, often you may want to learn a particular skill or technique and would be wiser to buy the information directly from an expert than to go to a seminar and listen to the speech of the same expert.

Here is the way I can prove this point. If a three-day seminar will require your driving to a different location, spending the night in a motel, eating out, and paying a registration fee to hear a particular expert, chances are you will save more money by setting up an appointment and paying a taxidermist to teach you individually for one day. This is why: Your first expense is the amount of money you could have earned if you had stayed at home and worked in your shop for three days. Add to this cost the depreciation on your car, gas and oil expense, motel bills, food, and the price of the seminar. When all these costs are totaled, you may find hiring the expert for a day is less expensive.

Any time you can pay money to learn how to improve your craft so you can charge more for your work or learn how to produce new products that will bring you added revenue, the money is well spent. You will continue to earn additional income from your taxidermy business.

For instance, if you glean but one money-making idea from the purchase of this book, then that idea will more than justify the cost of the book. Knowledge and information are two commodities to be bought and sold. And the enterprising taxidermist can make money by selling and purchasing knowledge.

(66) TAXIDERMY AS A REHABILITATION TOOL. The art of taxidermy is a rewarding, creative craft that makes the taxidermist very satisfied once a specimen is completed. Taxidermy has a therapeutic as well as a monetary value. Taxidermy is adaptable to almost any handicap a person may have.

Deer-foot gun racks, hat racks, jewelry, and even mounted specimens can be completed by the blind or legally blind. People in wheelchairs or those missing limbs can not only learn taxidermy but become proficient in it. Individuals with mental disabilities can study and perform well many of the aspects of taxidermy.

Taxidermy is limited only by a person's ability to learn or perform. For this reason, taxidermy is an excellent tool for vocational rehabilitation. Often taxidermists fail to earn extra income in their chosen profession because they do not realize its adaptability to other professions. And such is the case in training the physically and mentally impaired. By investigating the vocational rehabilitation possibilities in your area through county, state, federal, and private agencies, you may unlock the door to a rewarding and profitable business of teaching taxidermy to the handicapped.

This way to make more money in taxidermy will require research and study on your part. You may want to begin at your local library to find out what agencies around your home are involved in vocational rehabilitation. Also check with hospitals and insurance companies to determine if there are private agencies responsible for vocational rehabilitation in your region.

Time spent in teaching taxidermy to the physically and mentally impaired can represent a sizable income to the taxidermist in search of new dollars in his profession. I have worked with physically impaired students and have seen remarkable success. I am proud of their accomplishments and the quality of work they produce.

(67) MUSEUMS CAN MEAN MONEY. Exotic, beautiful, and different animal specimens are the downfall of most taxidermists. We mount some specimens just to prove to ourselves that we can. We mount others because they are lovely or unusual. Eventually a taxidermist may have more than one display room full of his favorite specimens.

To solve the problem of what to do with specimens, some taxidermists have created their own museums. Often these museums will be part of the taxidermy shop, while some may be housed in a separate building next to or close to the work area.

Taxidermists with a museum can charge a fee for viewers to visit the museum. Then each year the taxidermist can continue to add new specimens so that patrons will want to continue to visit the museum on a regular basis to see the new work.

The museum can be advertised through the taxidermy business. Comments like, "You ought to see the huge trophy deer we have mounted in our museum," or "Have you ever seen a life-size mount of a brown bear? We've got one in our museum," will draw taxidermy customers willing to pay a price for admission to your museum.

Another excellent method to bring money into your museum and customers into your taxidermy business is to let school children visit your museum at a reduced rate. Whole classes can visit. Some of these students will have relatives who hunt. The children either will bring back these relatives to see the museum or bring in specimens to be mounted.

There are some start-up costs involved in building your own museum, but the museum does not have to be extravagant. After the first year of operation, you can use some of the proceeds from the museum to enlarge the facilities and provide more specimens for the public to see.

(68) ENDANGERED AND PROTECTED SPECIES. There are federal laws against mounting endangered and protected species of birds and animals. Taxidermists will not mount these specimens for fear of stiff penalties and jail terms. However, these specimens may be mounted for display in museums, schools, and other public places with a federal permit. So the enterprising taxidermist who is looking for a way to generate more income will search out educational institutions eager for protected or endangered species and willing to go through the red tape required to receive federal permits.

Museums are also another source of revenue for the taxidermist. Often museums are willing to accept species and contract with taxidermists to mount specimens to place in their museums. Sometimes hunters going on safaris outside the United States will agree to take certain species of animals for a particular museum. These sportsmen will then kill the animals, pay the taxidermist to mount them, and donate the specimens to the museum as a tax write-off. So by contacting hunters prior to their leaving on safari, agreeing to do the work for them, and locating a museum that will be willing to accept their specimens once you have completed mounting them, the taxidermist provides a new source of income and a service to fellow outdoorsmen and museums.

(69) HOME TANNING CREAM. Each winter I receive from 20 to 50 telephone calls from all types of people, including retired people and Cub Scouts, who want a recipe to tan the skins of deer or other animals. Most of the time these novice tanners want a quick, easy solution to a very laborious task. Until recently I have told these callers to telephone the library and get a tanning recipe. However, there is a new solution now to the age-old tanning process that will permit the novice tanner to preserve his skin with a minimum amount of effort while still producing a fairly pliable hide. This product is Tannit and is sold commercially by Jonas Bro., Inc., Denver, CO 80203. A one-pound can of Tannit sells for $19.95 and can be resold to your customers for whatever mark-up you choose to place on the product. Tannit is all that is required to tan a skin. First, the hide has to be fleshed, salted, and allowed to dry. Then, once the tanning cream has been heated up in a double boiler, it is applied to the skin and worked in by using the edge of a kitchen table or a 2' x 4'. All the instructions for using Tannit are explained simply on the side of the jar. This may be a novice tanner's best solution to tanning problems.

Some commercial taxidermists also are utilizing this cream to tan scalps and hides which they are mounting. However, a new source of revenue—selling the jars of Tannit to customers who want to process their own hides—may be the best way to use this product to your advantage. Once processed according to the instructions, skins tanned with Tannit can be very supple and retain a high luster on the hair.

(70) MINIATURE MONEY MARKET. Although life-size fiberglass fish represent a good market for the enterprising taxidermist, the miniature market may be even larger. Miniature bass, trout, and salmon as well as great white sharks, sailfish, marlin, and striped bass are available for purchase for the taxidermist wanting to make extra income.

One of the best markets for miniature fiberglass fish reproductions is the tournament angler. Beautiful miniatures atop glistening trophies make the award more than just another piece of brass to sit in the corner. With all the bass clubs around the country awarding trophies for tournaments, the miniature bass that crowns the trophy is in high demand. Saltwater tournaments—where sharks, tuna, sailfish, king mackerel, tarpon, wahoo, and other species of saltwater fish are caught—offer an opportunity for the taxidermist who can unlock the mystery of the miniature.

The first big mystery in using miniature fiberglass fish is where to acquire them. The answer is Jamar Wildlife Studio, 117 N.W. 27th Ave., Ft. Lauderdale, FL 33311. The next big mystery comes in figuring out how to paint the fish. This problem is solved by purchasing the

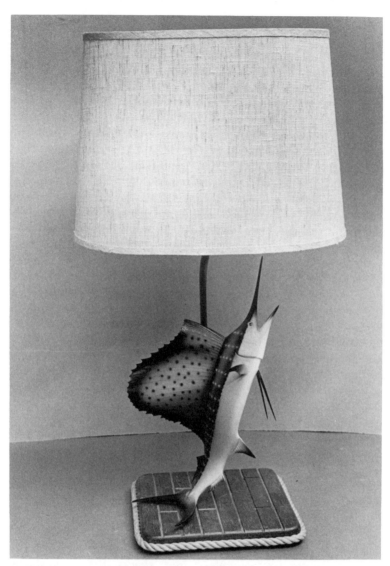

Good things in small packages also apply to the taxidermist who deals in miniatures such as this sailfish and lamp display. These can be good sellers for restaurants, craft shops, tourist stores in fishing resort areas, or simply the big-game angler who doesn't have the wall space for a full mount.

specimens already painted, unless you want to paint them yourself.

Even if you do not want to get into the trophy business you still are not locked out of the miniature market. Lamps featuring a miniature fish mount with a driftwood base will retail for $150.00 and up. The fish alone, on a finished driftwood base, will sell for as much as $130.00 to $140.00. Wall lamps are another possibility for the miniatures. These make especially attractive mounts if you live in an area that has sailboats or yachts close by.

One of the most popular items in the miniature market is a pen and pencil set with a miniature in the center. This is often an ideal trophy or award to be presented to a sportsman and also an item to be bought on impulse in your shop. A more expensive item is a wall clock with some type of miniature affixed to it. There is no limit to the number of items that can be produced from miniature fish. The profits that can be derived from this money-making opportunity make looking into miniatures a must.

For example, the miniature fish by itself, already painted, will cost $5.00, while ready-to-paint fish sell to taxidermists for $35.00. The cast alone costs $28.00, and lamps with miniature specimens of fish on a wooden base are $75.00. Now look at the suggested retail price. The painted fish by itself sells for $90.00. If you add a nameplate to any of these items the product can sell for even more. If the money has your attention, look at the wide range of specimens available:

Species of Freshwater Fish

Largemouth bass	8"
Brown trout	8"
Rainbow trout	8"
Atlantic salmon	11"

Species of Saltwater Fish

Great white shark	17"
Blacktip shark	12"
Blacktip shark	16"
Hammerhead shark	12"
Hammerhead shark	16"
Mako shark	14"
Tiger shark	12"
Tiger shark	16"
Yellowfin tuna	11"
Yellowfin tuna	7"
Blackfin tuna	11"
Blackfin tuna	7"
Bluefin tuna	11"
Bluefin tuna	7"
Allison tuna	11"
Sailfish	10"

Sailfish	16″
White marlin	10″
White marlin	16″
Blue marlin	19″
Broadbill swordfish	17″
Kingfish	11″
Wahoo	11″
Bull dolphin	11″
Striped bass	11″
Striped bass	7″
Bonefish	6″
Bonefish	8″
Tarpon	16″
Tarpon	9″
Bottlenose porpoise	11″
Bottlenose porpoise	6″

Once the taxidermist has the miniatures in hand, the next problem is where to sell them. This is not really a problem because most taxidermists should know where to market a product before they ever invest in the raw materials. Here are a few marketing techniques that may work for you in your specific area:

1. *Seacoast.* If you live around a seacoast area, a wide range of markets are available to you for saltwater miniatures. The first and easiest, of course, are gift shops that tourists frequent. But do not overlook restaurants and other attractions where large groups of people will see your work. Marinas usually conduct some types of fishing tournaments. Contact the tournament director six to eight months before the tournament is to be held. Show him your miniatures on trophies, ashtrays, pen sets, and lamps. Then offer to sell him engraved trophy plates for the winners in each tournament category.

2. *Freshwater Regions.* Very few locations in this country have not been touched by either the bass phenomenon or the trout-fishing bug. Clubs that compete for and attempt to propagate both species. Taxidermists can serve both groups of sportsmen with the miniatures. Miniatures can be used as trophies for tournament winners, or they can be presented to sportsmen who have done an outstanding job in the field of either trout or bass conservation.

3. *Catch and Release.* There is a growing movement in this country for sportsmen to release fish that they do not intend to eat or mount. Outdoorsmen often are awarded prizes or trophies for this catch-and-release program. Many a sportsman would like to have some

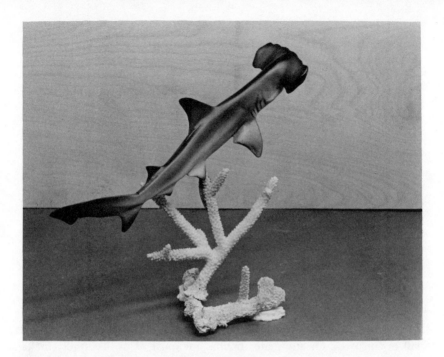

Lug a full-size hammerhead shark into the house and the next trip you make might be to divorce court. Sell your customers instead on a miniature with perhaps a small plate describing the catch. Even if you don't have a customer who actually caught a braggin'-size fish, there are plenty who like to collect these items. A series of sharks, trout, upland birds, etc. can be an important part of your line.

form of remembrance of the big fish he freed to fight again. This remembrance can be a miniature fish mount attached to a wall plaque with the name of the sportsman who released the fish, the date the catch was made, the approximate weight of the trophy, and the place the fish was caught. In this way, the sportsman has this trophy to remind him, even though the fish is free. This philosophy is becoming more and more prevalent with saltwater tournament anglers, bass-fishing clubs, and trout-fishing clubs. And the sportsman who releases his catch has a right to display a trophy signifying his accomplishment. The taxidermist who provides miniatures meets a very real need in this market.

The miniature market is easily adaptable to a wide range of products, awards, and home furnishings. Once again, if the taxidermist will identify a specific need, develop a miniature fish mount to meet that need, and convince customers that the miniature makes an award or product more valuable, he may very well find a very lucrative way to make more money in taxidermy.

One caution about the growing number of miniatures offered for sale by suppliers: Some may be quality products, but the vast majority I have seen are inferior products that do not pay attention to specific details. The rubber and plastic miniatures with which I am familiar lack the lifelike appearance of the fiberglass miniatures Jaymar Studios produces. So even though the fiberglass miniatures are more expensive than rubber or plastic models, I believe that the taxidermist who goes with quality will continue to have customers. But the taxidermist who attempts to supply inferior, cheaper miniatures always will be looking over his shoulder for the competitor with the better product.

Conclusion

The art of taxidermy is the re-creating of fish and wildlife from dead specimens to lifelike mounts. Taxidermy in the purest sense of the word will not provide an adequate income for most of us. To really make money in taxidermy you must become a salesman as well as a craftsman. You must be resourceful and look at your skills not as an end in themselves but as a beginning point to branch out into other related fields so you can draw income from all. To put more money into your business, you will have to do more than put a sign out in front of your shop and mount specimens for the people who happen to bring them by. You will have to be constantly wondering, "What else can I do with these animals and fish?"

You will need to attend seminars, workshops, and taxidermy conventions and seek the advice of others rather than being content with what you already know.

The taxidermy profession is a very rewarding vocation. There are always new challenges and opportunities. Thousands of dollars can be made by the taxidermist who is resourceful, creative, and innovative. If this book does nothing more than cause you to look at the opportunities you have at hand, then it will be well worth the price you pay for it.

APPENDIX
Important Addresses

BELT KITS

Tandy Leather Co.
9784 Pkwy. E
Birmingham, AL 35215

BOOKS

*Communicating the Outdoors
Experience*
Outdoor Writers Association of
America
3101 W. Peoria Ave.
Suite A-207
Phoenix, AR 85029

Photographer's Market
Writer's Digest Books
9933 Alliance Rd.
Cincinnati, OH 45242

The Synonym Finder
Rodale Books, Inc.
Emmaus, PA 18049

Photographer's Market
Writer's Market
Writer's Digest Books
9933 Alliance Rd.
Cincinnati, OH 45242

CUSTOM GARMENTS

Custom Coat Co., Inc.
227 N. Washington St.
Berlin, WI 54923

Licardo Gloves
27 Montgomery St.
Gloversville, NY 12078

W.D. Place Co.
Hwy. 60 W
Hartford, WI 53027

DEERSKIN GLOVE EXCHANGE

W.D. Place Co.
Hwy. 60 W
Hartford, WI 53027

FISH, MINIATURE FIBERGLASS

Jamar Wildlife Studio
117 N.W. 27th Ave.
Ft. Lauderdale, FL 33311

FUR COATS

Beca Furs
Rt. 1, Box 2
Sturgis, MS 39769

GAME FARM BIRDS

Wildlife Harvest
Rt. 1, Box 28
Goose Lake, IA 52750

HAT MAKING

Beca Furs
Rt. 1, Box 2
Sturgis, MS 39769

Fortman Bros.
N. Rt. 668
Rt. 1, Box 213
St. Mary's, OH 45885

INDIAN CRAFTS

Indian Trader
Box 867
Gallup, NM 87301

INSTANT MOUNTING FLUID

Touchstone Taxidermy Supply
Rt. 1, Box 5294
Bossier City, LA 71111

MAGAZINES

American Taxidermist
P.O. Box 11186
Albuquerque, NM 87192

Modern Taxidermy
Greenfield Center, NY 12833

Taxidermy Review
747 Santa Fe Dr.
Denver, CO 80204

Taxidermy Today
119 Gadsden St.
Chester, SC 29706

Wildlife Harvest
Rt. 1, Box 28
Goose Lake, IA 52750

Writer's Digest
9933 Alliance Rd.
Cincinnati, OH 45242

MOUNTAIN MEN ASSOCIATIONS

American Mountain Men
P.O. Box 259
Lakeside, CA 92040

National Association of Primitive
  Riflemen
Box 885
Big Timber, MT 59011

National Muzzle Loading Rifle
  Association
Box 67
Friendship, IN 47021

OUTDOOR FILMS

American Fishing Tackle
  Manufacturers Association
2625 Clearbrook Dr.
Arlington Heights, IL 60005

Bass Anglers Sportsman's Society
  (BASS)
1 Bell Rd.
P.O. Box 17900
Montgomery, AL 36141

National Rifle Association
1600 Rhode Island Ave., NW
Washington, DC 20036

National Shooting Sports
  Foundation
P.O. Box 1075
Riverside, CT 06878

PATCHES

Ted Salters
EBSCO Industries
Outdoor Division
1301 First Ave. N
Birmingham, AL 35203

PLASTIC MOLDS

Deep Flex Plastic Molds, Inc.
P.O. Box 11471
Fort Worth, TX 76110

QUAIL JEWELRY

Frank O. Hill
Pine Hill Game Farm
Rt. 5, Dept. WH
Union, SC 29379

SAUSAGE SEASONING

A.C. Legg Co.
P.O. Box 12083
Birmingham, AL 35202

SKULLCAPS

San Angelo Co., Inc.
P.O. Box 984
San Angelo, TX 76902

TAILS—WHERE TO SELL THEM

Adirondack Taxidermy Studios
Greenfield Center, NY 12833
(deer tails only)

Passloff, Inc.
28 W. 38th St.
New York, NY 10018
(deer tails only)

Sheldon's Inc.
P.O. Box 508
Antigo, WI 54409
(squirrel tails only)

TANNERIES

American Fur Dressing Co.
10816 Newport Hwy.
Spokane, WA 99218

Beca Furs
Rt. 1, Box 2
Sturgis, MS 39769

Clearfield Taxidermy
603-605 Hannah St.
Clearfield, PA 16830

Colorado Fur Tanning and Fur
   Dressing Co.
1787 S. Broadway
Denver, CO 80223

E.L. Heacock Co., Inc.
117 Bleecker St.
Gloversville, NY 12078

New Method Fur Dressing Co.
131 Beacon St.
South San Francisco, CA 94080

TAXIDERMY SUPPLY SOURCES

Bill Allen
Rt. 940
White Haven, PA 18661

Arco Taxidermy Supplies
Box 693
Tarpon Springs, FL 33589

Burnham Bros.
P.O. Box 100
Marble Falls, TX 78665
(knives and sharpening devices)

Chandler's Mounting Panels
206 Eisenhower St.
Jackson, MS 39209

Dan Chase Supply Co.
Rt. 2, Box 317A
Baker, LA 70714

Clearfield Taxidermy
603 Hannah St.
Clearfield, PA 16830

Commonwealth Felt Co.
160 Fifth Ave.
New York, NY 10016

Continental Felt Co.
22 West 15th St.
New York, NY 10011

Creative Woodworking
John Warden
2316 Ninth, NW
Birmingham, AL 35215

J.W. Elwood and Co.
Omaha, NE 68102

Engraved Nameplates
P.O. Drawer 375
Fairfield, AL 35064
(nameplates only)

E.L. Heacock Co.
117 Bleecker St.
Gloversville, NY 12078

Jonas Bros., Inc.
Denver, CO 80203

Knopp Bros.
N. 6715 Division St.
Spokane, WA 99208

Mackrell Taxidermy, Inc.
Concordville, PA 19331

McKenzie Supply Co.
P.O. Box 480
Granite Quarry, NC 28072

Meyer Fish Mix
4783 N. Bend Rd.
Cincinnati, OH 45211

Nippon Panel Co.
South Williamsport, PA 17707

North Star Freeze Dry
Box 439
Pegout, MN 56472

Archie Phillips
200 52nd St.
Fairfield, AL 35064

L.M. Rathbone
Star Rt. A, Box 769 E
Austin, TX 78746

Reel Trophy
P.O. Box 19085
Portland, OR 97219

G. Schoepfer
134 W. 32nd St.
New York, NY 10001

Taxidermy Supply Co.
5011 E. Texas
Bossier City, LA 71111
(Instant Mounting Fluid)

Touchstone Taxidermy Supply
Rt. 1, Box 5294
Bossier City, LA 71111
(Instant Mounting Fluid)

Van Dyke Supply Co.
Woonsocket, SD 57385

Wilderness Supply Co.
5118 Tulane St.
Jackson, MS 39209

Index

131